BLACK ENGLISH

EDUCATIONAL EQUITY'AND THE LAW

BLACK ENGLISH

EDUCATIONAL EQUITY
AND THE LAW

EDITED BY JOHN W. CHAMBERS, JR.

WITH A FOREWORD BY JULIAN BOND

1983

KAROMA PUBLISHERS, INC., ANN ARBOR, MICHIGAN

CONTENTS

FOREWORD

When United States District Court Judge Charles W. Joiner required the Ann Arbor, Michigan School District to recognize that some school children spoke "Black English," he widened a continuing controversy in American education.

This volume illuminates that controversy and guides the serious scholar toward deeper understanding of the Ann Arbor decision, the research to date which helped create it, and the efforts made since Judge Joiner's ruling in 1979 to use this at-home language as a basis for at-school achievement.

The essays that follow place "Black English" in historical, legal, international, pedagogical, and academic contexts; summarize more that two decades of research; and suggest how the accumulated knowledge might be used to help the forgotten actors throughout the controversy—Black youth shunted aside by a too-rigid system which equates Black English with ignorance.

Since *Brown v. Board of Education of Topeka,* in 1954, the United States has promised an equal education to all its children.

Most of our national efforts to make *Brown* real to date have concentrated on physical integration of students and staff and equalizing spending per pupil among schools.

The Ann Arbor decision requires an additional effort, and this book explains how costly ignoring that promise of '54 further may be.

JULIAN BOND

PREFACE

John W. Chambers, Jr.

A federal court in Ann Arbor, Michigan ruled in July, 1979 that the city's public schools were denying Black elementary school students their civil rights by failing to teach them to speak, read, and write standard English as an alternative to the Black English that was their native dialect. The result, the court said, was that the children were being denied an equal opportunity to succeed in school — and by implication, in later life.

Black English is the indigenous language of many working class Black people in the United States. Its history can be traced to the colonization of Africa and the opening of the slave trade. Both events brought various African languages into contact with English and other European languages (Bickerton, 1980). Black English is therefore not synonymous with "broken English," "ungrammatical language," "slang," or "street talk." Like all language, it is systematic and rule-governed in its syntax (grammar), phonology (sound system) and semantics (system of meaning). Although Black English is similar to the standard dialect of the business and market-place, the differences are rule-governed and not merely errors in the use of the standard dialect. Based upon linguistic criteria, Black English is recognized as one of the many dialects of English language used in the United States.

As the descendents of African peoples are under siege, so too is their language. Black children of Ann Arbor's Green Road section are typical of many children throughout the United States who are confronted with an assault on their culture and humanity. While the pathology that perpetrates this siege is understood by many, its effects are nonetheless pervasive in its destructiveness to Black children. Public education is one of the most influential Western institutions; it has historically shaped Black children's potential by destroying or underutilizing innate ability and creativity. This is accomplished by convincing children that they cannot talk, cannot communicate, cannot learn and achieve, and most of all, that they do not have the capacity to develop any of these skills. Language has either con-

sciously or unconsciously served as a whipping horse to rationalize motivat-
ions behind inhibiting the development of Black children. Even though the
issue of language is but one aspect of a larger historical socio-economic problem, it is explicit and tangible enough to bear the whip.

Alleyne (1980) describes the peculiarities of African-English contact,
and the political struggle and the language shifts undergone by African descendents in the United States, the Caribbean, and much of the Western hemisphere:

> 1. The surrender of the native African language is more rapid than is usually the
> case. The plurality of native languages in the New World, the inability of any one of
> them to assert dominance over the others, and the extreme differences in control of
> power between two communities in contact are the factors which led to the rapid
> surrender of the native language.
>
> 2. Learning conditions are generally inadequate for the effective adoption of the
> new language — e.g., no formal institutions, such as schools, exist for a long time,
> and even when they do come into existence, they remain inadequate (even to the
> present day).
>
> 3. A large group (the majority) is virtually excluded from any close contact with
> the new language and has virtually no motivation to make a complete adoption due
> to the absence of social and economic mobility. These factors continue over a long
> period of time and, in some cases, to the present and therefore preserve a large
> number of persons (constituting a significant social group) showing the most incom-
> plete adoption of (or the greatest deviancy from) the new language shift.
>
> 4. Subjected to the most extreme form of oppression and having no significant
> social interaction outside their own group, these persons develop a strong ethnic
> identity. There are acts of maroonage (Bush Negroes, Maroons, establishment of re-
> mote mountain communities after emancipation in Jamaica); and yet today, there
> is evidence of cultural maroonage, i.e., resistance to complete adoption (or accultur-
> ation). Political maroonage leads to the emergence of new languages (e.g. Saramacc-
> an, Sranan), cut off from any other language system. Cultural maroonage, in places
> like Jamaica and the United States, leads to the preservation of different degrees of
> approximation to the norm of the new language, including, in the case of Jamaican
> and Gullah, varieties commonly referred to as creoles, in spite of extensive, costly,
> and elaborate programs currently in effect to teach standard English (pp. 220-1).

These are just a few of the historical and linguistic conditions that have
created school systems throughout the United States which, like Ann Arbor's,
refuse to educate Black children. No single individual should alone bear the
brunt of being racist; what is at issue here is a racist policy that is institutional
in scope and deeply embedded in American culture. Racism, it seems, is the
"American Way."

Given the pervasiveness of institutional racism in the United States, it is not at all surprising that the court's ruling in the Ann Arbor Black English case was so widely misunderstood. The news media, operating under faulty, largely preconceived notions of race, contributed to the public's misinterpretation of Judge Joiner's decision. Media reports, for example, gave the impression that the judge had ordered that children be taught in Black English.

Nothing could be farther from the facts. Rather, the court clearly stated that children be taught to read in "the standard English of the school, the commercial world, the arts, the sciences, and the professions" (see Appendix). It also ruled that the schools take note of the fact that language used at home and in the local community is a barrier to students' learning only when teachers do not understand it and do not incorporate it into their method of instruction.

The purpose of the Ann Arbor conference, funded by the National Institute of Education and at which the papers published in this volume were first presented, was to provide a synthesis and an overview of current research in the instruction of children who speak non-standard vernacular English. This synthesis of current research and program development was intended for program administrators, curriculum and program development specialists, reading teachers, content area teachers, parents, and others who make use of its findings to develop effective programs of instruction. This information is critically important for the accurate assessment of individual needs and abilities and for placing children in programs that will maximize their intellectual potential and personal development accordingly. It is also useful to state and local agencies concerned with the development and implementation of more equitable policies. Although the conference at which the following selected papers were first given took place three years ago, these statements remain timely; the problems still exist, still require analysis and demand solution—perhaps even more so now than three years ago in the light of sporadic shifts to resegregation and the genesis of the magnet school concept in some areas of the country.

Vernacular Black English has been the subject of more research than most other English vernaculars and provides a natural catapult for the study of language variation and instruction generally. While vernacular Black English was the focus of discussion at this conference, the educational implications and principles derived from these papers are generally applicable to any group whose language has been stigmatized by our society, and for whom negative staff attitudes and practices result in unequal educational opportunity.

Language has been identified as a primary link between the child and the educational system. Children whose language is similar to the language of instruction generally benefit more from the educational setting than children who speak a non-standard vernacular of the language of instruction. The objective of a large portion of the research on language and education presented in these pages is to demonstrate a causal relationship between the language children bring to the instructional setting and their educational achievement. Several papers challenge the assumption that language variation must be a barrier to educational instruction, a challenge also mounted by the plaintiffs in the Ann Arbor Black English case. Other papers explore alternative ways of depicting the relationship between language, instruction, and achievement, as well as alternative methods of investigating these questions.

The Black population of the United States is historically unique, for the vast majority of its ancestry migrated to the American continents under conditions of chattel slavery. Centuries of slavery and pervasive racism have created negative attitudes toward, and low expectations for, the education of Blacks. For many years it was illegal to educate Blacks. From that time to the present, the education received by non-white minorities in general, and Blacks in particular, has not been of the same quality as that available to the white majority. Educational institutions have played a vital role in supporting a caste-like system based on race which serves the economic interests of the affluent. In such a system, individuals are placed in social and economic roles that are determined more by racial and ethnic background than by demonstrated competence and ability.

Because the low socio-economic position of non-white minorities is usually accompanied by the use of a language vernacular or dialect, some educational theorists have concluded that lower-class status is caused by "inferior" language that "deviates" from the "standard" English used in the marketplace. This conceptual framework, formally known as the *deficiency model*, has been used by political and cultural leaders to explain and maintain Black underachievement. Social scientists have used the model uncritically as a guide to designing research and interpreting data.

The papers contained in this volume demonstrate the hidden assumptions and erroneous reasoning implicit in the deficiency model. An alternative conceptual framework, the *difference model*, assumes that minority groups use their own cultures, that their cultures embody behaviors and strategies which result in instructional competencies different from those recognized by the dominant culture, and that minority children fail in school because educators do no recognize these children's culturally-specific competencies and therefore utilize inadequate learning theories, teaching methods, and methods for accurately assessing aptitude and achievement (Boykins 1978; Gibson 1976; Ramirez and Castenada 1974). The Ann Arbor Black English decision is of special significance because it incorporated the difference model into the legal structure. Judge Joiner held that, "The courts cannot find that the defendant school district has taken steps ... to provide [the teachers] with knowledge about the children's use of a 'Black English' " or to "suggest ways and means of using that knowledge in teaching students to read."

In addition to the problem of inadequate theories and models, Black and other minority children's formal education is impeded by another factor: the benefits of education and of applying oneself to school-related tasks are not fully reflected in the economic and social status of minority adults. Children often learn more from the behavior patterns of significant others (via modeling) than from classroom instruction. In far too many instances, verbal expressions of high educational aspirations are inconsistent with what is actualized by adult models. Thus, when parents tell their children that if they study hard they will be rewarded with a good job, parents may, at the same time, be transmitting to their children the impression that they really *do not fully believe this* because education has not paid off equitably for them. Ogbu corroborates this point: "The educational dilemma of subordinate minorities (Blacks) is that their children are expected to work as hard as whites in school for fewer ultimate rewards from society . . . Faced with the educational dilemma, subordinate minorities apparently choose to stop working in school since they could neither expect more for their work nor force society to change its discriminatory practices" (Ogbu 1974:13). Educational reform alone cannot solve the socio-economic problems faced by minority students. But, insofar as educational institutions are part of the social context of children's lives, efforts to alleviate social disparities in the classroom may contribute to improvements in other social arenas.

The conference from which the following papers were selected reviewed the innovative and promising directions research and program development are taking in the area of language variation in education. Participants included teachers, teacher trainers, linguists, sociolinguists, psychologists, and curriculum and program development specialists. All hoped to close the gap between theory and practice; the fruits and frustrations of their efforts are presented here.

While educational issues remained the central focus of the conference, participants were sensitive to the perspectives and perceptions of the general public. Research may discover potentially effective strategies, but successful implementation requires an active and joint effort between parents, communities, local, state, and national educational agencies, and teacher-training institutions. This book is offered as a contribution to the dialogue that must necessarily take place among all those parties. The very serious questions addressed at this conference were not initiated in the educational arena, nor will they be fully answered by experts in the field. Ultimately, education poses political questions: "Who will be educated, how will they be educated, and for what purpose will they be educated?" These are issues we all must decide.

All of the papers appearing in this volume, except that by Bailey, were prepared for the conference, Meeting the Educational Needs of Students Who Speak a Vernacular English in the Public School Setting, June 2-3, 1980. *The conference was funded by The National Institute of Education and co-sponsored by the Ann Arbor Public Schools. The final preparation of the manuscipts for publication was supported by the University of Maine at Augusta. Dr. Bailey's paper was presented at the National Invitational Symposium on the King Decision, sponsored by the Center for Black Studies, Wayne State University, February 21-23, 1980. His paper appears in* Black English and the Education of Black Children and Youth, *edited by Geneva Smitherman (Detroit, Michigan: Center for Black Studies, Wayne State University, 1981), pp. 94-129. Permission to reprint that paper here is gratefully acknowledged.*

EDUCATION AND THE LAW: THE *KING* CASE IN ANN ARBOR

Richard W. Bailey

Richard W. Bailey is Professor of English Language and Literature at The University of Michigan. He testified on behalf of the plaintiffs in the *King* case and has since written and spoken on the implications of the decision for teachers and school programs. He is a member of the Senior Advisory Panel in the Humanities of the United Negro College Fund. Among his recent publications are *Computing in the Humanities* (1982) and *English as a World Language* with Manfred Gorlach (1982). A collection of essays edited with Robin Melanie Fosheim, *Literacy for Life: The Demand for Reading and Writing*, is forthcoming.

Lawyers and educators share an interest in the relation of educational practices to the statuses and precedents that influence the struggle to maximize equal and effective education. In the Ann Arbor "Black English case" (officially *Martin Luther King Junior Elementary School Children et al. v. Ann Arbor School District Board, 473 F. Supp. 1371 [1979]*), both groups will find much to discuss that can lead to future action, but for the implications of the case to become clear, it is essential that both understand the general principles of educational litigation and the particular implications of that case and others that bear on the education of children and youth. In particular, they need to examine the issues that bear on the varieties of the English language, not only Black English, but also those that differ according to the region, national origin and social class of Americans.

Though it has been widely reported in the media, the *King* case has not always been clearly understood by those who have chosen to write and speak about it. It can easily be summed up, however, by saying simply that it concerned the task of teaching little children to read. Nothing in the decision nor in the plan devised by the Ann Arbor Schools in response to it has anything to do with the way people talk, nor is the case directed at the language styles a job-seeker might hypothetically use in seeking employment. Far from the threat to accepted practices that some have imagined, the case gets back to the basics, to the first of the proverbial three R's of schooling.

In other ways, this supposedly radical case is profoundly conservative. Presupposed by the Complaint for relief is the conviction that schools can accomplish the traditional goals of elementary instruction. The plaintiffs believe that the schools can do that job better, and thus, as Judge Charles W. Joiner wrote in his opinion, the case

> is a straightforward effort to require the court to intervene on the children's behalf to require the defendant School District Board to teach them to read in the standard English of the school, the commercial world, the arts, sciences and professions. This action is a cry for judicial help in opening the doors to the establishment (473 F. supp. at 1373).

Nothing in the underlying theory of the case can be viewed as an affront to the traditional aspirations of parents for their children, nor is there anything in it that threatens our democratic expectations that all citizens must be given access to the basic skills necessary for participation in the full range of our political, economic and social institutions.

In some instances, the case has been misunderstood by commentators who have sought to allocate blame for the circumstances brought to light by the trial. For a defendant to be found guilty, the court must specify the nature and occasion of wrong-doing, and naturally it did so in this case. But it is worth noting where the fault does not lie. It does not lie with the children: their language—Black English—does not constitute a handicap or a language barrier; it is the natural and systematic variety of English of their homes and peer groups. In itself, it does not present any special obstacle—or any special advantage—when these children begin to read. The fault does not lie with the parents of these children: their demand for action by the schools constitutes an ardent faith that schools can do better in teaching their children, and if a lawsuit is not as conventional as participation in P.T.A. meetings, it surely emerges from the same faith in the very great value of education. The fault does not lie with the teachers and administrators of the Martin Luther King, Jr., Elementary School in Ann Arbor. As the Court found, the "teachers do act in a responsible and rational manner to try to help the children" (473 F. Supp. at 1384). Despite all of the abundant evidence in Judge Joiner's opinion, it is easy to illustrate from the many news reports of the case that observers have variously blamed each of these groups: the children, the parents and the teachers.

Where, then, does the fault lie? In Judge Joiner's view, the failure was on the part of the defendant, the Ann Arbor Board of Education:

> The failure of the defendant Board to provide leadership and help for its teachers in learning about the existence of "Black English" as a home and community language of many black students and to suggest to those same teachers ways and means of using that knowledge . . . in connection with reading standard English is not rational in light of existing knowledge of the subject (473 F. Supp. at 1385).

It is here, then, that the significance of the Black English case becomes apparent: the Judge has found in the law an obligation on the part of Boards of Education to provide teachers with the best "existing knowledge" to assist them in realizing the goals of education.

It is particularly important to understand the implications of this case for teachers. For many years, various legislatures and community groups have turned to the schools to solve social problems of many kinds, not only in battering down racial barriers but also in responding to such reasonable demands as those of the handicapped for education in the mainstream, those of women and men to free our society of the irrational constraints of stereotyping by sex roles and those of cultural communities, set apart from the majority by the use of other languages, for programs of bicultural and bilingual education. As professionals and as caring human beings, teachers have generally welcomed each of these new obligations, but local communities (through their elected Boards of Education) have not always provided the support required for teachers to succeed: needs for special training and materials, specialized supporting staff and reduced pupil loads. Only in part, then, does the Black English case change the way that young Black children are taught in schools; its implications for teachers are great. If Judge Joiner's opinion serves as a precedent in other suits, it will surely be as a mandate for Boards and their professional administrators to provide "leadership and help" in a reasonable and rational way and to ensure that teachers are kept abreast of the continually accumulating knowledge that research brings to bear on the ways in which children grow and learn.

In considering the relation of education to the judicial process, most Americans do not regard the courts as the best forum for promoting change in teaching practices, and in the *King* case, Judge Joiner said explicitly that "it is not the obligation of this court to determine educational policy" (473 F. Supp. at 1391). Nonetheless, most Americans would agree that the courts must be available to citizens when other remedies fail to overcome the obstacles to equal educational opportunity. In the most significant educational decision by a court in our century—*Brown v. Board of Education of Topeka*—the Supreme Court voiced an eloquent statement of what must appear to be a fundamental principle:

> Today, education is perhaps the most important function of state and local governments. Compulsory school attendance laws and the great expenditures for education both demonstrate our recognition of the importance of education to our democratic society. It is required in the performance of our most basic public responsibilities, even service in the armed forces. It is the very foundation of good citizenship. Today it is a principle instrument in awakening the child to cultural values, in preparing him for later professional training, and in helping him to adjust normally to his environment. In these days, it is doubtful that any child

may reasonably be expected to succeed in life if he is denied the opportunity of an education. Such an opportunity, where the state has undertaken to provide it, is a right which must be made available to all on equal terms. (347 U.S. at 493).

Yet for all its eloquence in *Brown I*, the Warren Court did not raise education to a constitutional right. The Court's decision addressed only the question of *where* children would be educated: "Separate educational facilities are inherently unequal" (347 U.S. at 495). Not until 1973 did the Supreme Court address the constitutional issues of the quality of education itself. In *San Antonio School District v. Rodriguez*, a case brought to require that pupil expenditures be equalized between rich and poor school districts, the Burger Court retreated from a natural extension of *Brown:*

> We are in complete agreement with the conclusion of the three-judge panel below that "the grave significance of education both to the individual and to our society" cannot be doubted. But the importance of a service performed by the State does not determine whether it must be regarded as fundamental for purposes of examination under the Equal Protection Clause (411 U.S. at 41).

To do so, wrote the majority, would be to transform the Court into a "super-legislature," an inappropriate role in the view of the strict constructionalists, and hence they concluded that "education, of course, is not among the rights afforded explicit protection under our Federal Constitution. Nor do we find any basis for saying it is implicitly so protected" (411 U.S. at 44).

In his dissent (with Judge Douglas concurring), Thurgood Marshall correctly identified *Rodriguez* as "a retreat from our historic commitment to equality of educational opportunity and as unsupportable acquiescence in a system which deprives children in their earliest years of the chance to reach their full potential as citizens" (411 U.S. at 71). In Marshall's view, the right to an education is closely tied to the explicit constitutional guarantees protecting the right to free speech and the right to participate in the political process through voting. While the majority accepted the connection between education and the rights of speech and voting, it avoided Marshall's conclusion by saying that the Court "has never presumed to possess either the ability or the authority to guarantee to the citizenry the most *effective* speech or the most *informed* electoral choice." Yet the plaintiff children in San Antonio did not ask for a system that would make them "most" effective and informed, only for the opportunities given to children in wealthy districts to achieve their full measure of education.

Given the present composition of the Court, it seems unlikely that suits will soon prevail that attempt to form an implicit link between educational opportunities and the constitutional protection of speech and voting rights. At present, litigants must rely on a narrower range of guarantees:

(a) The Congress declares it to be the policy of the United States that—
(1) all children enrolled in public schools are entitled to equal educational opportunity without regard to race, color, sex, or national origin (20 U.S.C. 1701).

Yet the conditions that constitute "equality" of educational opportunity are still being defined. In the matter of funding, for example, the Congress has provided appropriations for districts where poverty is general; where poverty is restricted to a few—as it is in the King School district—schools are not eligible for funds provided for the "economically disadvantaged" under Title I of the Elementary and Secondary Education Act of 1965 or through state-funded programs of similar intent. What remains to be accomplished is a guarantee that each child, of whatever circumstances, be given access to the full range of educational opportunities.

In bringing the suit against the Ann Arbor School Board, the plaintiff children (through their lawyers) offered a series of arguments to expand the definition of "equal opportunity." While only the argument connecting their difficulties in school with "language barriers" (20 U.S.C. 1703 [f]) prevailed, it is worth recalling their primary assertion: "Plaintiffs have been denied an educational opportunity equal to that provided other students at King who are economically disadvantaged" ("Complaint for Injunctive and Declaratory Relief," p. 2). In support of this claim, they argued that "defendants deprived these children of such civil rights by failing to take into account cultural, social and economic differences between them and economically advantaged children at King School" (Complaint, p 16). By this line of argument, the plaintiffs attempted to enlarge the scope of the laws governing education beyond matters of "race, color, sex, or national origin" to issues involving "cultural, social and economic differences." But Judge Joiner was not persuaded by their arguments, and he ruled in December, 1978 that "this court does not intend to permit an expansion of the duty created by §1703 (f) to include elimination of what plaintiffs identify as cultural and economic barriers" (463 F. Supp. at 1030).

Despite the narrowing of the Complaint that necessarily followed the Judge's ruling, *King* did clarify a disputed issue that bears on the larger question of the remedies that plaintiffs may seek within the scope of the Equal Education Opportunity Act of 1974. In the view of the Board's attorney, the EEOA was designed to remedy only those "language barriers" found to exist in systems previously operating segregated schools. After reviewing the legislative history of the Act, Judge Joiner took note of President Nixon's message to Congress and, in his decision, quoted Nixon's expectation that "the statute should set 'standards for all school districts througout the nation, as the basic requirements for carrying out, in the field of public education, the

Constitutional guarantee that each person shall have equal protection of the laws.' " (473 F. Supp. at 1383; 118 Cong Rec. 8931 [1972]). On the presumption that Nixon intended to include *all* schools, Judge Joiner ruled against the argument that only districts manifesting "vestiges" of dual schools were encompassed within the statute.[1]

Even more important for future litigation is Judge Joiner's view—following *Lau v. Nichols* (414 U.S. 563) and other cases—that "the connection between failure to take appropriate action and race need not be in the form of an allegation of racially discriminatory effect" (463 F. Supp. at 1032).

Following Judge Joiner's ruling in favor of the plaintiffs on July 12, 1979, Ann Arbor school administrators responded immediately and vigorously by urging the Board of Eudcation to authorize appeal to the Sixth Circuit. Among many and varied arguments, Dr. Harry Howard (Superintendent of the Ann Arbor Schools) expressed apprehensions about the interference by the courts in the educational programs of schools. "I'm also concerned," he told the Board, "about the history of school districts under Federal Court jurisdiction. From then on, many of the actions are mandated by the Court with pressure from plaintiffs, and the school system is no longer operated by an elected Board of Education as our founding fathers intended it to be" (Board of Education meeting, 21 July 1979, transcript, p. 5). Later, in his final attempt to persuade the Board to appeal, Dr. Howard quoted Judge Joiner, though introducing the quotation as a reason in favor of appeal rather than as evidence of the Judge's opinion: "The courts are not the place to test the validity of educational programs and pedagogical methods" (Memorandum, Annex 80-182, 14 September 1979, p. 14; 473 F. Supp. at 1386). In short, Superintendent Howard led the Board to believe that local control and individual academic freedom could be maintained only through appeal and, he hoped, eventual reversal of the Judge's decision. But the majority of the Board was unpersuaded by Howard's arguments and voted not to pursue an appeal.

While the courts have intervened in educational matters in a variety of ways, only recently have decisions affecting the content of educational programs begun to emerge as an extension of decisions involving attendance districts, integration, evaluation of students and various obstacles to the exercise of First Amendment rights in schools. Though many believe the courts to be a natural source of relief when schools fail to promote free expression and sound education, there is also great reluctance by judges to preside over litigation involving the effectiveness of educational practices, even when such practices may be challenged on the basis of their discriminatory effect since such cases, as Dr. Howard claimed, seem to compromise the ideals of local control and academic freedom. In one such challenge, for instance, District Judge

Fred M. Winner ruled against a group of Latino students (who had requested a bilingual-bicultural education) and appended to his opinion a note candidly stating his views of such litigation:

> The recent proliferation of lawsuits against school districts, schools and school officials suggests that some people think that the courts should assume overall supervision of the nation's educational system, but I disagree, although I confess that I wonder if school personnel should not be awarded combat pay for their efforts in trying to educate in today's climate (*Otero v. Mesa County Valley School District No. 51, 408 F. Supp. 162 [1975] at 170*).

Of recent cases that have reached the Supreme Court, perhaps the most germane is *Bradley v. Milliken* (433 U.S. 267 [1977]), the Detroit desegregation case. Here the Supreme Court upheld the "remedial guidelines" specified by the District Court to reform educational practices involving reading, in-service training for teachers, testing and counseling and career guidance. "The content of the required program," wrote the Court in reference to the reading program, "was not prescribed by the [district] court; rather, formulation and implementation of the program was left to the Superintendent and to a committee to be selected by him" (433 U.S. at 275). Such an approach leaves local control and academic freedom intact, but only if the proposed new programs meet the test of reasonableness as a strategy for eradicating "the effects of past discrimination."

In Judge Joiner's opinion in the Black English case, the same principle of leaving education in the hands of professional school personnel was maintained, and it is worth noting that, as in *Milliken*, the design of the remedies was left in the hands of those who were responsible for the violations. Yet school policy-makers were not left free to do as they chose; as Judge Joiner wrote, "It is not the intention of this court to tell educators how to educate, but only to see that this defendant carries out an obligation imposed by law to help the teachers to use existing knowledge as this may bear on appropriate action to overcome language barriers" (473 F. Supp. at 1385). In so stating, the Judge made clear that "the test of reasonableness and rationality" is conditioned by the state of "existing knowledge" that bears on the design of educational programs:

> What action is appropriate should be judged simply in light of existing knowledge on the subject. If there is substantial existing knowledge on the subject that supports the position taken by the School District Board [in the plan submitted to take account of Black English], then this court's obligation is to find that the plan complies with the law (473 F. Supp. at 1397).

Such language clearly invites further testimony on the relation of "existing knowledge on the subject" to the proposed plan. In evaluating the plan drawn

up by Ann Arbor administrators to comply with Judge Joiner's order, the
plaintiffs agreed with the Board's use of "existing knowledge" and indeed
commended the Board and its administrators for their diligence and good
faith ("Response on Behalf of the Plaintiffs," 20 August 1979, p. 1). Yet the
plaintiffs also suggested a series of modifications to the plan that were clearly
related to expert testimony given at the trial, particularly in their suggestion
that "nothing in this plan shall be interpreted to allow for segregation of
Black students or the removal of such students during regular class hours of
instruction to accomplish the tasks of the Language Arts Consultant" ("Response, p. 3).Since Judge Joiner was firm in asserting the right of the Board to
determine the best use of "existing knowledge"—though he would not allow it
to be ignored—the plaintiffs were unsuccessful in having the plan amended to
comply with their recommendation.

In commenting on the several modifications of the Board's plan that were
proposed by the plaintiffs, Judge Joiner retreated somewhat from the position
of his earlier ruling:

> These matters might be quite appropriate for inclusion in a plan of the
> kind envisioned by the court's earlier opinion and might be considered
> appropriate had they been proposed by the defendant School District
> Board. However, it is not the obligation of this court to determine educa-
> tional policy. These matters involve a judgment regarding educational pol-
> icy. For the court to step in and make a determination on any of these
> matters would inject the court into the matters of educational policy not
> envisioned by the congressional enactment. There is substantial evidence
> in the record to support the decision of the School Board on the proposals
> made by the Board. Although there is also substantial evidence to support
> suggestions made by the plaintiffs, the educational policy is to be deter-
> mined by the School District Board. The law is to be intepreted by this
> court. If the proposals are rational in light of existing knowledge as estab-
> lished in this case, they should be approved (473 F. Supp. at 1391).

Evidently enough, the Judge reverted to his earlier claim of non-interference
and granted the Board the presumption of competence to select among competing theories of "existing knowledge." While the School Board retains the
privilege of superior expertise in determining the "appropriate action" that
follows from such knowledge, it is a privilege that can be challenged by others. Judge Joiner thus opens the possibility of adjudicating competing views of
"existing knowledge" and their practical implementation in the classroom.

In the context of the *King* Black English case and its implications for further litigation, four themes have so far been addressed: the obligations of
Boards to provide teachers with the results of "existing knowledge;" the relation of educational guarantees to Constitutional rights; the lack of remedies
when educational failures are based on "cultural, social, and economic differences;" and, the standard of "existing knowledge" as a measure of "rationali-

ty" of educational programs. Additional issues arising from the case involve the more specific issue of "home language" of the plaintiff children, Black English.

While the *King* case is the first in the Federal courts to recognize the structural and functional properties of Black English, earlier decisions implicitly note the distinctiveness of that language variety. In *Milliken*, for instance, the Supreme Court recognized some of the special circumstances that foster Black English:

> Children who have been thus educationally and culturally set apart from the larger community will inevitably acquire habits of speech, conduct, and attitudes reflecting their cultural isolation. They are likely to acquire speech habits, for example, which vary from the environment in which they must ultimately function and compete, if they are to enter and be a part of that community. This is not peculiar to race; in this setting, it can affect any children who, as a group, are isolated by force from the mainstream (433 U.S. at 287).

In commenting on the reading program required by the lower court, the Supreme Court found it appropriate that the variety of language typically found in the segregated schools of Detroit "must be treated directly by special training at the hands of teachers prepared for that task" (433 U.S. at 288). Such "speech habits" encompass both foreign languages—Spanish in Latino communities, Cajun French in Louisiana, or Chinese in the Chinatowns of New York and San Francisco—and any variants of language developed within the communities "isolated by force of law from the mainstream."

Those who foresaw the development of litigation involving Black English looked naturally to the Supreme Court's decision in *Lau v. Nichols* (414 U.S. 563).[2] As in *Rodriguez*, the Court stopped short of basing its decision on the Equal Protection Clause and instead invoked the protections of the Civil Rights Act of 1964 (42 U.S.C. 2000d). In reversing the lower court decisions, it acknowledged the obligation of the San Francisco schools to provide special help for the 1,790 Chinese school children who had "no knowledge of English" and who were not receiving any help in acquiring it from the schools. In so doing, the Court affirmed the legality of the regulation promulgated by the Department of Health, Education and Welfare in 1970:

> Where inability to speak and understand the English language excludes national origin-minority group children from effective participation in the educational programs offered by a school district, the district must take affirmative steps to rectify the language deficiency in order to open its instructional program to these students (35 Fed. Reg. 11595 [1970]).

For this line of argument to prevail in the case of Black English, however, plaintiffs would be obliged to argue that Black children command an entirely distinct language system and manifest an "inability to speak and understand the English language." Such a direction might have been followed in the Ann

Arbor case, and indeed one of the plaintiffs' contentions did suggest that direction in pointing to "linguistic interference due to two differing grammatical systems of what ostensibly appears to be the same language" ("More Definite Statement in the Form of an Amended Complaint," p. 7). But the distance between the application of *Lau* and the circumstances in Ann Arbor was simply too great for this direction to be a fruitful one. Indeed, after hearing testimony from the plaintiff children, Judge Joiner concluded:

> The teachers at King School had no difficulty in understanding the students or their parents in the school setting and the children could understand the teachers and other children in that setting. In other words, so far as understanding is concerned in the school setting, although there was initially a type of language difference, there was no barrier to understanding caused by the language (473 F. Supp. at 1381).

It could not in these circumstances be argued that the children were excluded from "effective participation in the educational programs" as the Chinese children had been in the circumstances brought to light by the *Lau* case.

In seeking a more fruitful line of argument, attorneys for the plaintiffs drew the Court's attention to that portion of the EEOA of 1974 that points to the consequences of "language barriers:"

> No state shall deny equal educational opportunity to an individual on account of his or her race, color, sex, or national origin, by—
> (f)the failure by an educational agency to take appropriate action to overcome language barriers that impede equal participation by its students in its instructional programs (20 U.S.C. 1703).

Yet even this tactic did not seem immediately promising, and in writing to invite comments of various educators and linguists in May 1979, the attorneys for the plaintiffs identified this portion of the statute as "an obscure provision of the Equal Educational Opportunity Act of 1974." Its obscurity was by no means illuminated by two cases in which it had been invoked. In *Guadelupe v. Tempe* (587 F. 2d. 1022 [1978], for instance, the appellants argued that the educational program formulated by the School Board in Tempe, Arizona, should be designed on bilingual-bicultural principles for an elementary school in which 544 of 605 students enrolled were of Mexian-American or Yaqui Indian origin. In ruling in favor of the Board, the Court noted that "the appellants do not challenge the appellees' efforts to cure existing language deficiencies" (587 F.2d at 1030) and ruled that there was no justification in the law for the claim that "appropriate action" must be bilingual and bicultural instead of the program of instruction in English that existed in the elementary school attended by the children. From the conclusions of the Appeals Court, it appears that no attempt was made by the appellants to evaluate the question of "appropriate action" in light of the state of "existing knowledge" concerning the most effective ways to educate children of the Mexican-American and Yaqui community.

A second case involving 20 U.S.C. 1703 (f) provided no more encouragement to the plaintiffs in the Black English case. In *Deerfield Hutterian Association v. Ipswich Board of Education* (468 F. Supp. 1219 [1979]), Chief Judge Fred Nichol was asked to adjudicate the demand of a community of Hutterites who wished the local School Board to establish an elementary school in which their children might be educated in their native language, Tyrolean German. Twenty-four of the thirty-five Hutterite colonies in South Dakota enjoy elementary schools where children can be taught in Tyrolean German and protected from the "worldly" values of the elementary schools where English is the medium of instruction and non-Hutterite children predominate. When the colony at Deerfield was established in 1971, the Hutterites refused to allow their children to attend the elementary school in a nearby town and demanded that the Board erect and maintain a school within the community. In ruling in favor of the Board, the judge left open the option that the Hutterites might educate their children privately within the colony, but he also noted--citing one of Judge Joiner's preliminary rulings in the Black English case (451 F. Supp. 1324 [1978]—"that there is no constitutional right to special educational services to overcome unsatisfactory academic performance based on cultural, social or economic background" (468 F. Supp. at 1231). As for the issues raised by the Hutterites under 20 U.S.C. 1703 (f), Judge Nichol did not find in the case any violations nor did he feel that the arguments introduced in invoking that statute were sufficiently strong to require more than summary dismissal in his written opinion.

With no record of successful litigation by plaintiffs wishing to demonstrate "the failure by an educational agency to take appropriate action to overcome language barriers," attorneys for the Ann Arbor children were obliged to develop a case in which the nature of the "language barrier" would be explained through expert testimony. The legislative history of the provision gave no clear guidelines for interpreting such terms as "appropriate action," "language barriers," and "equal participation," but it seemed to plaintiffs' counsel and their advisors that a case could be made that the Ann Arbor School Board was in violation of 20 U.S.C. 1703 (f).

When introduced by President Nixon in March 1972, the bill containing the language that eventually was enacted as 20 U.S.C. 1703 (f) had as its primary purpose the limitation of school busing as a remedy for school segregation, and naturally most discussion and debate concerned desegregation and Nixon's proposed "statutory limitation" designed to "curb busing." In his message to Congress accompanying the legislation in March 1972, Nixon did little more than paraphrase the provision touching on language barriers:

School authorities must take appropriate action to overcome whatever language barriers might exist, in order to enable all students to participate equally in educational programs. This would establish, in effect, an educational bill of rights for Mexian-Americans, Puerto Ricans, Indians and others who start under language handicaps, and ensure at last that they too would have equal opportunity (118 Cong. Rec. 8931 [1972]).

By emphasizing the intent of the President to remedy *whatever* language barriers might exist, Judge Joiner concluded that "the President's list of persons covered by his proposal is only merely illustrative but could well include students whose 'language barrier' results from the use of some type of non-standard English" (451 F. Supp. at 1332).

In hearings held later in March 1972 by the House Committee on Education and Labor, Congressman Victor V. Veysey took the opportunity to question HEW Secretary Elliot Richardson about the provision:

Congressman Veysey: Now, it seems to me that this is a new and affirmative concept in the law.

I would like to have your thinking behind that and what the implication of that particular section may be insofar as requirements on States and local educational institutions dealing with Spanish-speaking children, Chinese-speaking shildren, Indian-speaking shildren, and so on.

Secretary Richardson: This part of the legislation, Mr. Veysey, acknowledges that language barriers diminish the full benefits of educational opportunity for all children.

The central focus of this provision is on providing English language skills for non-English-speaking children. It gives renewed emphasis to the problems of unequal educational opportunity for national origin minority groups, first addressed in the Department of Health, Education, and Welfare memorandum of May 25, 1970, on national origins.

That memorandum requires schools with any substantial number of minority group pupils to provide them with English language training. It also prevents them from assigning such students to special education classes merely because of language deficiencies. It rests on Title VI of the Civil Rights Act of 1964.

So, the clause of this legslation to which you referred is essentially declaratory of what we have previously construed to be a Title VI requirement. The result undoubtedly of this Presidential initiative will be to step up bilingual programs. The States, of course, would have responsibility for ensuring that local educational agencies take appropriate action to overcome whatever language barriers may exist in their schools (Hearings on H.R. 13915, 27 March 1972, at 28).

Subsequent references to the provision during the hearings (e.g., pp. 115, 150) suggest that Secretary Richardson envisioned benefits for Latino students particularly, and the HEW Memorandum cited in his testimony speaks exclusively of the "inability to speak and understand the English language." Nonetheless, by asserting that "all children" may suffer from "language barriers," Richardson left open the possibility that a suit might be brought on behalf of children speaking a distinctive variety of English.

In developing the case during the trial, counsel for the plaintiffs elicited testimony asserting that language boundaries are defined by beliefs and attitudes as well as by differences in pronunciation, vocabulary and grammar. Communities of speakers may assert that two individuals speak the "same language" even when the language varieties they use are not mutually intelligible: Cantonese and Mandarin, for instance, are both regarded as varieties of "Chinese" even though speakers of one cannot understand or be understood by speakers of the other. Different communities, on the other hand, may regard quite similar varieties, ones that do not impede communication, as "different languages:" Yiddish and German spoken in Berlin presented such a case before the former language was virtually exterminated in that area between 1933 and 1945. With these facts in mind, it is easy to understand the aphorism of Max Weinreich—"A language is a dialect with an army and a navy" —and to grasp the intimate connection between language and social and political insititutions.

During the Black English trial, expert witnesses developed the argument that the language of the plaintiff children was characterized by a variety of structural features typical of the Black English current in Northern cities. Evidence in support of these descriptions came from tape-recordings of the children in their homes and also from the testimony the children themselves offered in the opening days of the trial. Thanks to Judge Joiner's instruction to the court reporter to "put it in the vernacular that comes out" (transcript, 13 June 1979, p. 7), the trial record itself illustrates the Black English used by the children. In summarizing both sources of evidence, Judge Joiner found that the children command a range of oral language skills:

> Their speech in court was highly intelligible and contained only traces of "Black English." This is true although the court heard tapes played of the same children in casual conversation in which talking among themselves their speech was a true "Black English" vernacular. In oral speech, though they seem to quickly adapt to standard English in settings where it appears to be the appropriate language (473 F. Supp at 1392).

Though sociolinguists would undoubtedly argue with the Judge's distinction between "traces" and "true" Black English, his summary of the situation does capture the variability of language features that characterize the range of styles employed by the plaintiff children.

Other cases have touched on the social dimensions of language varieties, but seldom has testimony explored findings of contemporary research so thoroughly as in *King*. In a New York desegregation case, for instance, the court noted the social and cultural isolation of impoverished groups and the relation of such isolation to language: "This difference in style and even in language between lower and dominant classes is a worldwide phenomenon creating serious teaching problems" (*Lora v. Board of Education*, 456 F. Supp. 1211 [1978] at 1259). Likewise, in a case that resulted in the overthrow of "tracking" by ability groups in Washington, D.C., the Judge recognized that "communication within the lower class environment, although it may rise to a very complex and sophisticated level, typically assumes a language form alien to that tested by aptitude tests" (*Hobson v. Hansen*, 269 F. Supp. 401 [1967] at 480). Yet such occasional observations have typically been limited to quite general summaries. In another New York case, the court identified issues that bear directly on the Black English issue:

> There are, of course, serious pedagogical issues facing the schools, as, what is the extent to which instruction of Black children should make use of a non-standard dialect and special experiences in teaching them to read or, should the classroom be used to induce the use of American standard dialect and acceptance of Middle class norms . . .
>
> These problems may, the court recognizes, be compounded where rich and poor, black and white, are integrated in public schools, bringing to the same classrooms different patterns of speech and varying life styles. But this is a problem—and an advantage—of a heterogeneous democratic society.
>
> There also may be some basis for the contention of some blacks that *some* white teachers expect black children to fail and, therefore, do not have the emotional ability to successfully teach them. But as already noted, segregation desired by blacks is no more acceptable than that enforced by whites . . .
>
> These problems of techniques are for school authorities. They have the broadest freedom to develop curriculae so long as illegal segregation is not utilized (*Hart v. Community School Board*, 383 F. Supp. 699 [1974] at 746-47; citations omitted).

What is important about such reviews of testimony and scholarship is that judges have recognized problems arising from language as matters for "school authorities," not for the courts. But with the enactment of 20 U.S.C. 1703 (f) and the precedent of the Black English case, they become matters for litigation.

While Judge Joiner found the Ann Arbor School Board guilty of failing "to provide leadership and help for its teachers in learning about the existence of 'black English' as a home and community language of many black students and to suggest to those same teachers ways and means of using that knowledge in teaching the black children" (473 F. Supp. at 1385), the "language barrier" was found to be in the attitudes of the teachers, even though they were highly trained and well-intentioned. And "since the language barrier was found to be a barrier on the part of the teachers, the court suggested that the plan should be directed at assisting the teacher" (473 F. Supp. at 1385).

For many years, educators have understood that teachers' attitudes and expectations are a crucial variable in the differing degrees of success of their pupils. Some have discussed such attitudes in terms of a "silent curriculum," the "Pygmalion effect," or "hidden agendas," and studies have accumulated that illustrate the force of such beliefs in the classroom. Even outside the domain of educational research, the importance of teachers' attitudes toward their pupils is generally recognized by the informed public. In the Kerner Report of 1968—the findings and recommendations of president Johnson's National Advisory Commission on Civil Disorders—this issue was cogently and prominently discussed:

> Studies have shown that the attitudes of teachers toward their students have very powerful impacts upon educational attainment. The more teachers expect from their students—however disadvantaged those students may be—the better students will perform. Conversely, negative teacher attitudes act as self-fulfilling prophecies: teachers expect little from their students; the students fulfill the expectation. As Dr. Kenneth Clark observed, "Children who are treated as if they are uneducable invariably become uneducable."[3]

Perhaps because "existing knowledge" is so well-established and abundant on the question of self-fulfilling expectations, Judge Joiner was led to his opinion that the Ann Arbor School Board had failed to meet the established standard of "rationality" and "reasonableness" by neglecting to make teachers aware of it.

Attitude studies directed toward language and the stereotypes associated with it reveal that nearly all Americans, Black and white, assign the most attractive qualities to voices that reflect "network English," a variety that encompasses a range of regional differences but has few traits that are overtly stigmatized in popular lore or usage handbooks. When other varieties are considered, most respondents give second place (after "network English") to the speech that most resembles their own. Hence Blacks give relatively high ratings to voices heard on tape that are identified as Black, and whites high ratings to voices perceived to be white. Such opinions, of course, are based on deeply embedded stereotypes, and a great variety of conclusions may follow as a consequence of the judgments of the listeners. When a national sample of teachers was asked to respond to such statements as "Black English is an inferior language system" or "When teachers reject the native language of a student, they do him great harm," they revealed a tolerance for language variation, and many were "favorably disposed" to Black English.[4] Results like these suggest two possibilities: that teachers recognize the "right answers" when asked to react to abstract principles about language varieties; or that they are genuinely sympathetic to language differences and recognize them as natural consequences of healthy diversity in American society.

The more specific question of attitudes among the King School teachers is especially difficult to answer since neither the depositions nor the testimony during the trial fully clarified their views of the Black English spoken by the plaintiff children. Had the expert witnesses been involved in a research project, they might have attempted to study these attitiudes in three ways: 1) the reaction of the teachers to statements of principle (e.g.,"The encouragement of Black English would be beneficial to our national interests"); 2) their reaction to unknown pupils observed through audio and video tape where opinions about the "promise" or "intelligence" of the children might have been e-licited; and 3) observation of the teachers' interactions with the plaintiff children (e.g., eye contact, verbal interaction, and "body language"). Since the preliminaries to the trial were based on the adversarial relation of a law suit, such organized research was not possible, and the experts were obliged to draw on much less evidence including statements and testimony by the plaintiff children (most of whom were quite favorable to their teachers), school records and sworn testimony of the teachers and school personnel.

Even before the opening of the trial, it was clear that the teachers were anxious about the litigation and reluctant to amplify their views about the plaintiffs and the issues arising from Black English. Some staff at King School did admit that the children from the Green Road housing project where the plaintiffs live were distinguished from other pupils by their language, and both the principal and the specialist teachers (including the school psychologist and the speech therapist) recognized the existence of "Black English" and believed that the plaintiff children were most comfortable in that variety. But the classroom teachers responded quite differently. Most refused to acknowledge the existence of Black English, and none of the classroom teachers said that they believed that special efforts were required in teaching the plaintiff children and their peers to read.

Only one classroom teacher amplified her views of Black English testimony, and her response suggests something of the dilemma as she and her colleagues perceived it:

Q. Have you ever taught a child in Ann Arbor who was most comfortable in black English or black vernacular English?

A. I don't know—I don't know how you're asking me that. I mean, I don't understand. What—

Q. All right. Have you ever taught a child in Ann Arbor who was most comfortable speaking in black English or black vernacular English?

The Court: What part of the question bothers you? The words "most comfortable"?

The Witness: Yes, I suppose so—

The Court: Pardon?

The Witness: Yes, I suppose that's what's bothering me. I—

The Court: You define that—what that means and then you can answer the question the way you want to. We want you to answer the question according to your terms. How you define it, unless Mr. Kaimowitz [Plaintiffs' counsel] instructs you otherwise.

The Witness: Well, the—the black English bothers me, a—

The Court: All right. That bothers you also. All right.

The Witness: —because I feel that I've heard the same kind of English spoken in the deep South by whites and so, therefore, the black English bothers me. I would say I have heard black children speak English that is—that I have heard spoken by whites, southern whites. I have heard black children add the S, the S onto words that were already plural. I have heard whites do the same thing. I have heard black children use the be verb, perhaps in the wrong place. But I guess I can't really say I find a black child is most comfortable with that.

    I think the black children that I've come in contact with actually know both. And—I don't know whether I can say they're most comfortable with it (Transcript, 19 June 1979, pp. 8-10).

After the trial, the attorney for the Board admitted that he had suggested that the teachers demand of plaintiffs' counsel (both in deposition and on the witness stand) a definition of "Black English," advice that may have made the teachers especially wary of the term. In responding to his advice—which the attorney later conceded might have been a strategic error—the teachers appeared to deny what the administrators and specialists had admitted, that the plaintiff children and others from their housing project were distinguishable by their language. But whatever the influences on their testimony, the teachers revealed to the Judge that they had failed "to take into account the home language system" (since most of them refused to acknowledge that such a "home language" existed) and thus by their testimony supported the claim that a "language barrier" separated them from their Black English-speaking pupils.

The plan formulated by school administrators and approved by Judge Joiner consisted of a variety of "appropriate actions" to aid the teachers in working with pupils whose home language is Black English, and the issues are perhaps best clarified by examining those objectives that bear directly on classroom practices. According to the plan, when King School teachers have completed the in-service seminars in June 1980, they should:

    a. be able, using a variety of informal techniques, to identify students in their classes who speak black English;

    b. be able to recognize specific problems encountered by individual black English speakers attempting to read standard English;

    c. be able, in the classroom setting, to distinguish between a dialect shift and a decoding mistake as a black English speaking student is orally reading from standard English material;

    d. have incorporated into their reading program appropriate language-ex-

    perience activities;
 e. use a variety of possible instructional strategies to help black English
     speaking students learn to read standard English (473 F. Supp. at
     1389).
Needless to say, in the course of developing these skills, the teachers will learn
a great deal about language and language attitudes as well as more specific information about the history and structure of Black English. Though the training program is still in progress, it appears that the teachers are adding to their
knowledge and finding new insights into both the structural detail and the climate of attitude and belief that surrounds language variation. One teacher, in-
terviewed in December, 1979, told a reporter:"I feel good about the ramifications. The more we can learn about our language and the dialects, the better
for us. We're learning a lot about how we feel about the language and how the
language affects us."[5]

    When the inservice program is completed in June 1980, the only test of
whether or not the "language barrier" found to exist at King School has been
"overcome" will emerge from the opinions of the teachers and staff members
who have pariticipated in the training. Unfortunately, because of the limited
scope of the inservice course and the relatively small number of Black English
speaking pupils at King School, there will be little opportunity to compare the
expected and the actual improvement of reading skills among the pupils.[6]
With the report of the "external expert consultant," based on observation and
interviews with the teachers, administrators will be in a position to declare the
training program a success or a failure, but since the consultant will not have
observed prior classroom practices at King School before the implementation
of the plan, there will be little objective data on which to base a conclusion.
Given the continuing reluctance of the administrators to admit that any "language barriers" have ever existed at the School, it seems unlikely that the final
evaluation will acknowledge any significant changes in educational practices
(though staff and teachers will certainly be congratulated for their diligence
and hard work). In the absence of objective data, the administration will be in
a position to qualify the degree of success with almost any adjectives of their
choice.

    From a legal point of view, the Black English case is not likely to have im-
mediate influence on other suits of a similar character.[7] As a lower court case,
it has precedential value only in the Eastern District of Michigan, and other
Boards are likely to defend themselves more vigorously than the one in Ann
Arbor saw fit to do, claiming that virtually any activities promulgated by administrators for the benefit of reading teachers constitute the "appropriate action" required by the statute. Just as Latino students have been generally unsuccessful in substituting bilingual and bicultural programs for allegedly inade-

quate attempts to overcome the language barriers of an unsympathetic school system,[8] so Black pupils are not likely to succeed in demanding any special programs that would assist them and their teachers in overcoming the "language barriers" that impede the effectiveness of reading instruction. Other groups whose dialect of English is stigmatized by their teachers are, of course, not eligible to bring suit under provisions of 20 U.S.C. 1703 (f) unless they can claim that discrimination is based on "race, color, sex, or national origin," Hence, white migrants from the Ozarks to an industrial city in the Upper Midwest, for instance, may suffer from similar language barriers, but they are not in a position to bring an action in Federal court for relief.

Insofar as *King* was a success for poor Black children, the effect of the decision will lie in the new practices introduced in educational programs, both those for teachers already in the classroom and in the language arts classes required of candidates for teacher certification. Though some have predicted a new wave of funding for basic studies of Black English, it seems more likely that the stimulus for research will lie in the domain of the attitudes of teachers and the consequences of those attitudes for the teaching of such basic skills as reading and writing. Many of the principles of language variation are now well-understood within the world-wide community of English speech, both from the perspective of structural variation in the language and from that of the beliefs and stereotypes that surround the variants. What remains to be accomplished is to make this "existing knowledge" available to teachers, most particularly teachers at schools like King with a diverse group of children who bring to the classroom a considerable range of different kinds of English.

Even though the issue of the "language barrier" created by teachers and other school personnel does not seem especially promising for future litigation, there are other trends in the courts that address the problems of Black children and youth in schools. Among the most promising are those suits that challenge the techniques by which pupils are assigned to one or another of the categories of "educable mentally retarded" (EMR), and when the Black English suit was first filed in June 1977, plaintiffs' attorneys alleged that "a disproportionate number of Green Road children have been labelled handicapped or recommended for placement in special education classes because of unsatisfactory academic performance" (Complaint, p. 11).[9] While this claim did not survive the first stage in the narrowing of the suit, it is worth noting the fate of the arguments supporting it since they point to issues successfully litigated in other cases.

Rule 13 of the Michigan Special Education Code (R 340.1713) provides the definition of "learning disabled" and includes a safeguard that should prevent the inappropriate labelling of children:

"Learning disabled" means a person identified by an educational planning and placement committee [EPPC], based upon a comprehensive evaluation by a school psychologist or certified psychologist or certified consulting psychologist or an evaluation by a neurologist or equivalent medical examiner to evaluate neurological dysfunction, and other pertinent information, as having the following characteristics:

(a) Disorder in 1 or more of the basic psychological processes involved in understanding or in using spoken or written language, which disorder may manifest itself in imperfect ability to listen, think, read, write, spell or do mathematical calculation.

(b) Manifestation of symptoms characterized by diagnostic labels such as perceptual handicap, brain injury, minimal brain damage, dyslexia or aphasia.

(c) Development at less than the expected rate of age group in the cognitive, affective or psychomotor domains.

(d) Inability to function in regular education without supportive special education services.

(e) Unsatisfactory performance not found to be based on social, economic or cultural background.

In the application of rule 13 (e)—the distinction between "learning disability" and "social, economic or cultural background"—the Ann Arbor schools were challenged in the Black English case.

In the first of his three rulings, Judge Joiner extracted from the Complaint "two interrelated theories" arising from the issue of "social, economic or cultural background:" a theory of equal educational opportunity and a theory of stigmatization.

Under the first theory, he identified two classes of children with educational problems: one composed of children with handicaps, as specified in rule 13—and the other with learning difficulties arising from their "social, economic or cultural background." In ruling on this issue, he found that there was no statute or precedent that would oblige schools to extend services beyond pupils with physical or psychological disabilities to those suffering the consequences of a "deprived" background, even if the difficulties encountered by the children were directly connected with the syndrome of poverty. In other words, there was no legal requirement that the schools bring the children such compensatory services that would make their opportunities equal to those of their economically advantaged classmates: "eyeglasses and hearing aids as necessary, newspapers, magazines, television program and film assignments, [and] trips" (Complaint, p 21). Even though special services of one kind were provided to the handicapped, there was no mandate to supply services of another kind to non-handicapped children whose difficulties in school arose from their "background."

Though the second theory—the "theory of stigmatization" was no more successful that the first, it touches on issues that have been successfully litigated elsewhere. Under this theory, the plaintiffs claimed that some children were wrongly identified as learning disabled (or some other category of special need) because the evaluation procedures had failed to discriminate genuine disability from behavior arising normally from the "social, economic or cultural background" of the children. As many studies have shown, children who have been classified as "special" often suffer grievous consequences:

> In psychological terms, to identify a child as retarded becomes a perpetual self-fulfilling prophecy, limiting the child's capabilities and opportunities. Studies indicate that once labeled and committed to classes for the retarded a child will act out a stigmatized role of a mentally retarded person; he comes to see himself as others see him.[10]

It was doubtless with this prospect in mind that the framers of rule 13 introduced section (e) to warn members of Educational Planning and Placement Committees against a diagnosis in which evidences of a pupil's "social, economic or cultural background" would be confused with the symptoms of brain damage or perceptual handicap. But though the procedures by which the children were labeled might be challenged in a Michigan court, the stigmatization theory lacked sufficient standing for a Federal decision; Judge Joiner ruled that it did not "state a claim upon which relief can be granted under the Fourteenth Amendment or under 42 U.S.C. §§1983 and 1985(3)" (451 F. Supp. at 1329). An additional obstacle to the pursuit of this theory in the case arose from the fact that none of the parents of the plaintiff children had appealed the decision of an EPPC even though the opportunity for such appeals is provided in the Special Education Code. Yet, when special placements are recommended by school professionals, "the typical parent will have no familiarity with the type of evidence needed to contest the placement" (71 Mich. L. Rev. [1973] at 1245), and only one of the parents of the plaintiff children refused the offer to have a child designated as "learning disabled."

Because the lines of argument emerging from the placement of the plaintiff children in EMR programs failed early in the suit, there was no opportunity to explore the possible bias of these procedures when the case came to trial. When asked about tests for EMR placement and those more generally used to measure progress in learning, the school administrators avoided certain crucial issues that might have been central to explaining the difficulties the plaintiff children faced at King School. In response to interrogatories about test results of white and Black children at King, for example, the attorneys for the Board replied that "test data according to racial categories are not maintained by the Ann Arbor School District" (Answers to First Set of Interrogatories, p. 57) After the decision, a diligent Ann Arbor reporter discovered that such data was indeed available in computer records but that the former Director of Research and Testing (now a school superintendent elsewhere in Michigan) had not "run" the data to provide the answers. Hence, correlations between race and test results were indeed "maintained" even though they had not been compiled to allow an answer to the interrogatories about white and Black children at King School. The reporter also discovered that the Director of Research had studied some of the data "on his own time" and for supposedly personal research. In his inquiry, the connection between poverty, race and low test scores was firmly established: "students whose family income was 'below median' averaged 75% as many right answers as those whose family income was 'above median.' " Black children from single parent homes were found to be reading at the 18th percentile on nationally normed test. White children living with single parents were reading at the 63rd percentile.[11]

In light of such findings, it is inevitable that future litigation will continue the attack on the possible racial, economic and cultural bias of tests. A landmark case dealing with this issue has, of course, recently been concluded in California. In 1972, in *Larry P. v. Riles* (343 F. Supp. 1306), Judge Robert Peckham issued a preliminary injunction to prevent the state of California from using IQ tests to determine EMR placements; his action was challenged in the Court of Appeals on the ground that the denial of IQ tests would impose an unfair burden on the schools and make it difficult to identify retarded children but the appeal failed (502 F. 2d 963 [1974]). Eventually, in October 1979, Judge Peckham found that the "placement mechanisms operate with a discriminatory effect that effectively forecloses a disproportionate number of black children from any meaningful education" (43 LW 2298 [1979]). The tests, though validated for a large group of students, had not been validated for "each minority group with which they are used." In the Judge's view, "an inference of discriminatory intent is inescapable" (48 LW 2298 [1979] at 2299).

Aptitude tests of various kinds have long been suspect, even when the scores are only a part of the process by which children and youth are placed in special programs or denied admission to schools and colleges. Perhaps the most thorough judicial review of the shortcomings of such tests is provided in *Hobson v. Hansen* (269 F. Supp. 401 [1967]) where litigants identified the bias of such tests against minorities and the poor. In general, scores can reflect a whole variety of unintended variables: the sex and race of the test administrator, the degree of enthusiasm for school and school values in the home, the kind of curiosity about the world fostered in the community and the individual variances in health, alertness and attitude that may be present in a particular administration of the test.[12] But perhaps paramount of the variables that are not connected with a child's true ability and potential are those that reflect language. As noted in *Hobson*,

the skills measured by scholastic aptitude tests are verbal. More precisely, an aptitude test is essentially a test of the student's command of standard

English and grammar. The emphasis on these skills is due to the nature of the academic curriculum, which is highly verbal; without such skills, a student cannot be successful (269 F. Supp. at 478).

Even tests that purport to measure non-verbal skills (e.g., spatial relations or abstract reasoning) depend upon the student's ability to understand and respond to directions given in that variety of English recognized as "standard" in the school setting.

Professionals in the testing industry have not been indifferent to the challenges presented in litigation and in the scholarship and popular media. Many tests have been re-validated to represent a greater diversity of students, and questions that call for information narrowly available to middle-class children have been eliminated. But many tests, especially those designed for young children or for persons not able to read, include items that depend on linguistic reception or production and thus may favor or penalize certain groups of test-takers. In the Wepman Auditory Discrimination Test, for example, children are asked to say whether pairs of words read by the test administrator are the "same" or "different." Among the forty pairs presented in this test is the supposed contrast of *pin* and *pen*, a distinction unlikely to be made by a Black English test-giver (and hence not detected by non-BE test-takers) or, in the reverse case, a distinction unlikely to be heard by a BE child however carefully articulated by the test-administrator. Consonant contrasts contained in the Wepman   test include *sheaf/sheath* and *clothe/clove* which will similarly bias "auditory discrimination" and enhance the likelihood that a Black English-speaking child will be identified as a person needing speech therapy or some other form of "intervention."

Even more elaborate tests of auditory discrimination may produce discrimination by dialect. The Goldman-Fristoe-Woodcock Test, like the Wepman used in testing some of the plaintiff children at King School, employs a standard tape stimulus to reduce the variant pronunciations of different test administrators. By rotating the order in which a set of words is presented, the test-maker hopes to elicit successively the ability of children to discriminate such contrasts as:

    core, coal, comb, cone (items 30, 32, 53, 64)
    pat, pack, path, patch (items 39, 56)
    cat, cap, catch, cab (items 32, 77)

For the Black English-speaking child, some of the words within each set may be heard as homophones: *cove* and *coal*, *comb* and *cone*, *pat* and *pack*, and *cat* and *cap*. Even though this test was validated to include scores from the "culturally deprived," it seems not to have occurred to its makers that there might be some reason other than deprivation for the low scores of that group of children.

One additional test may serve to show how Black English may be an important factor in the scores received by certain children. In the Illinois Test of Psycholinguistic Abilities, as in several other tests of its type, children are shown pairs of line drawings and asked to complete a sentence read by the test administrator describing differences between the first drawing and the second. In the following extracts from the test, the italicized portion shows the place where the child's response is invited; the answers here supplied are all included in the scoring manual as answers that are to be treated as "incorrect:"

    5. Here is a dress.
        Here are two *dress*.
    6. The boy is opening the gate.
        Here the gate has been *open*.
    7. The bicycle belongs to John.
        Whose bicycle is it? It is *John*.
    14. [The boy] wanted another cookie but there weren't *none/ no more*.
    22. Here is a foot.
        Here are two *feets/foots*.
    29. The boy had two bananas.
        He gave one away; he kept one for *hisself*.
    31. Here is a child.
        Here are three *chilluns*.

Whatever such a test may measure, it certainly does not provide any useful information about the "psycholinguistic abilities" of young Black English-speaking children.[13]

Even though a great deal is known about the structure of Black English and other varieties of American English, tests which depend for their success on productive or receptive language skills seem to be constructed without any reference to possible bias that would penalize persons whose English differs from that of the test maker. A Californian, for instance, might design a test that would presume that such pairs as *collar/caller* and *Don/dawn* were the "same" with the result that most children in the North Central states would be scored wrong on the item; conversely, a test maker who presumes that a contrasting vowel in these pairs is a part of "standard English" will succeed in failing nearly every child west of the Mississippi River! While it is clearly possible to produce tests of auditory discrimination or psycholinguistic ability that are free from bias favoring or disfavoring certain normal varieties of English, there seems to have been little energy devoted to making them.

The *King* case is likely to produce reforms in the training of teachers, the study of teacher behavior in the classroom and the formulation and administration of standardized tests. That these reforms have long been needed is obvious, not only from the research that bears on each of them but also from the abundant discussion of such matters in legal opinions and rulings. *King* has given educators and informed citizens across the nation an opportunity to consider the facts of language variation in our country and the consequences of these facts for teaching little children to read.

In a broader context, the Black English case and others like it address the profound issues of national unity and of our willingness to accept the cultural and liguistic diversity that characterizes our society. In ruling against the request of Spanish-speaking students in Tempe, Arizona, for bilingual and bi-cultural education, the Court of Appeals for the Ninth Circuit addressed this question of diversity and found in it a threat to the "social compact" that makes our unity as a society possible:

> Our analysis returns us to the foundations of organized society as manifested by the nation-state. We commence by recognizing that the existence of the nation-state rests ultimately on the consent of its people. The scope of this fundamental compact may be extensive or limited. Its breadth fixes the limits of government by the nation-state.
>
> Linguistic and cultural diversity within the nation-state, whatever may be its advantages from time to time, can restrict the scope of the fundamental compact. Diversity limits unity. Effective action by the nation-state rises to its peak of strength only when it is in response to aspirations unreservedly shared by each constituent culture and language group. As affection which a culture or group bears toward a particular aspiration abates, and as the scope of sharing diminishes, the strength of the nation-state's government wanes.
>
> Syncretism retards, and sometimes even reverses, the shrinkage of the compact caused by linguistic and cultural diversity. But it would be incautious to strengthen diversity in language and culture repeatedly trusting only in syncretic processes to preserve the social compact. In the language of eighteenth century philosophy, the century in which our Constitution was written, the social compact depends on the force of benevolence which springs naturally from the hearts of all men but which attenuates as it crosses linguistic and cultural lines . . . Multiple linguistic and cultural centers impede both the egress of each center's own and the ingress of all others. Benevolence, moreover, spends much of its force within each center and, to reinforce affection toward insiders, hostility toward outsiders develops. (*Guadelupe v. Tempe Elementary School*, 578 F .2d 1022 [1978] at 1027).

Such is the conventional view that unity must spring from uniformity and that diversity must eventually devolve into a weak confederation of mutually distrustful communities. Yet diversity exists despite more than a century of effort to "Americanize" differences and "standardize" linguistic and cultural values. If the *King* Black English case has importance beyond the education of children, it is in the way in which it confronts the contradictions of the welfare of the nation-state and the well-being of its citizens in asserting their just demands to equal opportunity.Those who fear diversity see in it a threat to our efforts to work together in the "social compact." Those who have faith in the power of benevolence to transcend the narrow concerns of one's own community welcome it.

NOTES

1. In a review of the legislation prepared for the conservative American Enterprise Institute in 1972, Professor Robert H. Bork of Yale (soon to be appointed as Solicitor General by President Nixon) warned the Congress that the provisions for "equal opportunity" were not limited to systems where "dual schools" had been maintained: "Since these subsections do not explicitly refer to a forbidden segregatory intent, it would be possible to interpret them as imposing obligations upon schools that have never practiced *de jure* segregation" (*Constitutionality of the President's Busing Proposals* [Washington, D.C.: American Enterprise Institute, 1972], p. 20).

2. See, for instance, Tyll van Geel, "The Right to be Taught Standard English: Exploring the Implications of Lau v. Nichols for Black Americans," *Syracuse Law Review* 25 (1974), 863-910.

3. *Report of the National Advisory Commission on Civil Disorders* (New York: Bantam Books, 1968), p. 429.

4. See Orlando L. Taylor, "Teacher's attitudes toward Black and Nonstandard English as Measured by the Language Attitude Scale," in *Language Attitudes: Current Trends and Prospects*, eds. Roger W. Shuy and Ralph W. Fasold (Washington, D.C.: Georgetown University School of Language and Linguistics, 1973), pp 174-201. Statements of general principles involving the connection of attitudes of teachers and the success of their pupils are widely available. For instance, Jane W. Torrey concluded that "within the social context, minor differences in structure can take on enough symbolic importance to be construed by black children and teachers alike as alien and therefore threatening. Changing the attitudes of teachers toward black English and the attitudes of black children toward standard English will not in itself solve the problem of urban education, but it will almost certainly have to be a part of any considerable improvement in school effectiveness" (*Harvard educational Review* 40 [1970] : 258). For a thorough survey of the extensive scholarship on this issue, see Karen L. Greenburg, " Teachers' Attitudes toward Language Variation" (New York: N.Y.U. School of Education, February 1977).

5. Katherine Green, "Black English Ruling's Impact Subtantial," *The Ann Arbor News* (16 December 1979), p. A-4. Three King School teachers amplified their views of the training program at the conference held in Ann Arbor in June, 1980. All three said that their knowledge of Black English had been increased and that they had come to recognize more explicitly the importance of sensitivity to language and its use. Dr. Thomas Pietras, director of language arts for the Ann Arbor Schools, was quoted as saying "I feel sincerely we've done a good inservice . . . All students are benefiting and certainly the teachers are too." (Roger Le Lievre, "Black English Course Helped, Teachers Say," *The Ann Arbor News*, 4 June 1980, p. 3-A.

6. It is not entirely clear just what techniques will be used to measure growth in reading skills. On September 10, 1979, Dr. Eugene W. Thompson (Office of Research and Evaluation, Ann Arbor Public Schools) offered the following appraisal in a document subsequently presented to the Board as supporting evidence for Dr. Howard's recommendation in favor of appeal:

> It is, of course, recognized by any reputable educator that it is not possible to conclude via established research procedures that any measured alteration within one school year in the reading skills of seven plaintiff children are the result of an inservice program designed to modify staff attitudes. It is certainly possible to measure gains in reading skills. However, to consider the two variables as dependent and independent within the span of less than nine months is folly (Materials for School Board meeting of 19 September 1979, Annex 80-182, p. 22).

On October 5, 1979, however, Dr. Thompson recommended that scores be gathered for the pupils identified as Black English speakers on the California Achievement and Michigan Educational Achievement Program tests:

> As data are reported to the Research and Evaluation Office, they will be accumulated and reported by group averages. These averages will be compared to the overall Ann Arbor and King School data. Inclusion of these data in the final evaluation report will be the success factor.

7. Teachers in Houston who pass an "English language competency test" will become eligible to teach in a special after-school program designed to assist Black students; teachers who fail the test will participate in a "free remedial program" to improve their skills. Introduced as part of an out-of-court settlement in a desegregation case, this plan was apparently influenced by the Black English trial in Michigan. See the *Houston Chronicle*, 13 November 1979, p. 1. The *objective* of the Houston "extended day" program is to provide minority students with "competence" in "standard English;" the proposed teaching strategy draws on the contrastive techniques developed for instruction in English as a second language and appears to emphasize oral skills.

8. An exception is *Citron v. Brentwood Union Free School District* (455 F. Supp. 57 [1978]); see also *United States v. Texas Education Agency* (532 F. 2d 380 [1976] at 398).

9. Of the fifteen plaintiff children in 1977, three were found eligible for services as "learning disabled" and two were identified as "emotionally impaired." During the 1976-1977 school year, when the suit was being prepared, six of the fourteen students at King School receiving special education services were Black. At that time, about 13% of the students enrolled at King were Black, 7% Asian and Latino, and 80% white.

10. "Segregation of Poor and Minority Children into Classes for the Mentally Retarded by the Use of IQ Tests," *Michigan Law Review* 71 (1973), p. 1219.

11. Anne Remley, "Behind the Black English Case," *Ann Arbor Observer* (December 1979), p. 22.

12. Recent studies of test bias are summarized by Meyer Weinberg, *Minority Students: A Research Appraisal* (Washington, D.C.: HEW, 1977), pp. 57-59. *School Psychology Digest*, vol. 8, no. 1 (Winter 1979) is devoted entirely to varying views of the same sub-

ject.

13. Though generally discredited, the ITPA is still in widespread use, though not in Ann Arbor schools. See *The Eighth Mental Measurements Yearbook* (Highland Park, N.J.: Gryphon Press, 1978), pp. 573-83. Both the Wepman and Goldman-Fristoe-Woodcock are commonly used with children suspected to need speech therapy. See the reviews in the *Yearbook*, p. 1451 and pp. 937-38 respectively; dialect bias is not mentioned in these otherwise thorough discussions of the tests. In the *Expanded Manual for the Peabody Picture Vocabulary Test* (1965), another test used in Ann Arbor and administered to some of the plaintiff children, Lloyd M. Dunn admonishes testers to use care in pronouncing words intended to stimulate the child to point out which of four drawings represents the thing named: "It is extremely important for the examiner to know the correct pronunciation of each of the words to be administered. *Webster's New Collegiate Dictionary* (G. & C. Merriam, 1953) has been used as the authority" (p. 5). Presumably it is also important for the examiner to know something about the normal child's notion of "correct pronunciation," but this possibility is not mentioned. If the *examiner* is not comfortable with the dictionary pronunciations, some leeway is provided: "where colloquial or other local pronunciations are accepted in a community, these alternatives may be used along with the dictionary preferences" (p. 6). The success of this test will depend upon the administrator's awareness of the "community" to which the child belongs and the standards of pronunciation "accepted" within it.

RECOGNIZING BLACK ENGLISH IN THE CLASSROOM

William Labov

Dr. Labov is a Research Professor at the Center for Urban Ethnography, University of Pennsylvania, Philadephia, Pennsylvania. Dr. Labov has conducted extensive research in the areas of sociolinguistincs and language patterns of non-standard English speakers. Dr. Labov is a past president of the Linguistic Society of America, and presently the Associate Editor of *Language in Society*. He is co-editor of a series on Quantitative Analysis in Linguistic Structure published in 1979.

The Ann Arbor decision must be considered an important step in the effort to achieve racial integration of American society. In recognizing Black English as a linguistic system, Judge Charles Joiner, Jr. acted to bring teachers and Black children closer together, arguing that teachers should have a better knowledge of the resources children bring to school. He also brought together linguists and educators: an immediate consequence of the Ann Arbor decision is that linguists must do a better job of making their research findings available to those who need them. This presentation is intended as an effort to organize our present knowledge of Black English in a form that will be useful to designers of reading programs.[1]

Research on Black English was begun by Black scholars particularly conscious of Black people's African heritage and the resemblance between the language used in the Caribbean and the Black speech forms of the United States. Lorenzo Turner's research on the African elements in Gullah (1949) and Beryl Bailey's description of Jamaican Creole English (1966). provide an excellent foundation for the study of inner-city Black dialects. This type of research began in the mid 1960's, a time when violent protests throughout the country called attention to high levels of unemployment and a low degree of educational success in the cities. My own work in Harlem, funded by the Office of Education, was concerned with the issue of reading failure. The biracial team of researchers addressed two main questions:

1. How great were the difference between the linguistic systems used by Black and white youth in the inner-cities?

2. Do language differences contribute to the reading problems of Black

children in inner-city schools?

If the Ann Arbor case had emerged at that time, the court would have found very little agreement among linguists. There were violent controversies between traditional dialectologists and students of Caribbean creoles, particularly on the historical origins of the dialects spoken in the United States. The dialectologists argued that Blacks spoke regional dialects no different from white speakers of the same southern region. Those familiar with the creoles of the Caribbean argued that Black English was a creole language with an underlying structure very different from other dialects and quite similar to the Caribbean English-based creoles. Dialectologists traced features of Black English to British dialect patterns; creolists maintained that those features were derived from a general American creole with Caribbean roots and ultimately from African grammar and semantics.

On the second question, the causes of reading failure, there was even less agreement. Most psychologists endorsed the verbal deprivation theory: that the language of Black children was impoverished as a result of deficiencies in their early environment (Deutsch, Katz, & Jensen; 1968). An alternative view developed, partly as a result of the alleged failure of enrichment programs, that lack of educational success was attributable to genetic defects in certain children (Jensen, 1969). Linguists and anthropologists as a whole disagreed with both of these views. They argued that Black children had very rich verbal resources which remained untapped because of ignorance on the part of children and teachers.

One might have expected the Ann Arbor Black English trial to become a battleground for these opposing points of view. One would think that the defense could find psychologists and linguists who would argue that there was no such thing as Black English, or that it was only a regional dialect, or that it was just the bad English of non-standard speakers. But this did not happen. There were no witnesses for the defense. The plaintiffs presented Joiner with a consistent testimony that appeared to represent the consensus of all scholars involved in the study of Black English and its educational implications. Although there was disagreement, the defense attorneys, who did a tremendous amount of research on the question, could not find anyone who would support a significantly different position.

How did such a remarkable consensus come about? Three distinct streams of events leading to this result can be identified. First, having weighed the evidence advanced by the other side, linguists and dialectologists achieved a certain consensus by the time of the trial. Second, the existence of Black English became recognized as a social fact, partly through the legitimation of the Black experience and of the term *Black*, and partly through the publication of such books as Dillard's *Black English* (1972). Third, a new generation of young Black linguists entered the field in the 1970's: John Baugh, Mary Hoover, John Rickford, Milford Jeremiah, Jerrie Scott, Geneva Smitherman, Arthur Spears, Anna Vaughn-Cooke, and many others. Their research has deepened our knowledge of Black English and its educational implications. For all these reasons, the testimony given at the trial carried far more weight than if the proceedings had taken place ten years earlier.

Judge Joiner's summary of the evidence (1979) was a model of clarity in its treatment of the general character of Black English, the relationship between Black English and other kinds of English, and the historical origins of this language variant. He saw clearly that Black English is a distinct linguistic system but that it is not a foreign language, that it has many features in common with southern dialects since most Blacks lived in the South for several centuries, and that it has distinct marks of an Afro-Caribbean ancestry, reflecting the earlier origins of the Black community. Joiner concluded that the law must therefore recognize a distinct linguistic form historically derived, in part, from Black people's heritage of slavery and segregation.

Joiner was not as clear on the details of these linguistic differences, on how Black English interferes with reading, or on what can be done to overcome any such interference. The opinion lists the twelve features of Black English that figured most prominently in the testimony. As it now stands, this list is not likely to be very useful to teachers who want to know if the children in their school use Black English, or to curriculum writers who want to take it into account in building reading programs. Yet the testimony did include many of the elements that we need for these purposes. The aim of this paper is to reorganize the descriptions of Black English presented at the trial into a form that will be more useful to teachers and educators.

With the trial over, Black English grammar is seldom discussed. A great deal of attention has been paid to the teachers' attitudes toward the use of Black English in their classrooms, and to children's attitudes toward the use of standard English. Judge Joiner himself concluded:

> If a barrier exists because of the language used by the children in this case, it exists not because the teachers and students cannot understand each other, but because in the process of attempting to teach the children how to speak standard English the students are made somehow to feel inferior and are thereby turned off from the learning process (1979, p. 6)

This was not the trial's original orientation. At first the judge had ruled out consideration of cultural and political factors, and insisted on an exact description of the *linguistic* barriers in question.[2] My own testimony was accordingly aimed at the grammatical description of the language used by Ann Arbor Black children, showing that it was the same as the Black English vernacular used in New York, Washington, Chicago and Los Angeles. I then presented evidence showing structural interference with the use of the alphabet and other steps in reading. The defense lawyers appeared to have read most of my written work, including unpublished galleys. They asked how I could reconcile my testimony with the earlier conclusion (Labov, Cohen, Robins, & Lewis, 1968; Labov & Robins, 1969) that structural differences between Black English and standard English could not in themselves account for massive reading failure. We had concluded that the principle problem was a cultural and political conflict in the classroom and that Black English had become a symbol of this conflict.

I responded to the defense's query with three main points. First, we know more about the structural differences between Black English and standard American English than we did ten years ago due largely to research conducted by Black linguists in the 1970's. Second, there is no reason to think that educational programs informed by popular attitudes alone can make major imrovements in the teaching of reading. Teachers need to incorporate concrete information on the features of Black English into their daily lesson plans. Finally, the contradiciton is only apparent since negative attitudes can be changed by providing people with scientific evidence of the language's validity.

Judge Joiner's opinion indicates that he may not have accepted this point of view. He did accept an educational program, initiated by the Ann Arbor Board of Education, designed to change general attitudes. No reading curriculum has yet been established using information on Black English.[3]

The gap between general discussion and concrete practice has not gone unnoticed. At a symposium on the outcome of the trial held in February, 1980, Benjamin Alexander, President of Chicago State University, argued that Black English was obviously a myth, since no one had been able to describe it to his satisfaction. At the conference held by the NIE in June, 1980, a teacher at the King School agreed that her attitude towards Black English may have been improved by the new training program, but said that she had not yet had instruction on what to do when faced with a child who had not learned to read.

This paper will apply our present linguistic knowledge to the teaching of reading. It will present not merely a list of Black English features, but a coherent view of its linguistic system that is accessible to non-linguists. I will then indicate how this system may interfere with the business of learning to read standard English, and where in a reading method this information may be taken into account.

1. Terminology

Throughout the trial, the term "Black English" was used to refer to the vernacular system that was the home language of children living in the Green Road housing project, and to the system used by the majority of American Black people in their casual conversation (Joiner, 1979, p. 12). It is normally used in quotes by the judge, who notes at the outset two equivalent terms: "Black vernacular" and "Black dialect." *Black English* will undoubtedly remain the most commonly used term following Dillard's book (1972) of that title.

For more precise discussions, I prefer to apply the term *Black English* to the entire range of linguistic forms used by Black Americans. The term *Black English Vernacular* or BEV will be used to refer to the grammar used by children growing up in the Black community and by adults in the most intimate in-group settings.[4] *Standard Black English* refers to the speech forms used by educated Black speakers in formal and public situations. It contains phonological variation from standard forms, but the same standard English syntax. There are, of course, many intermediate forms, but no intermediate system has been identified clearly enough to deserve a separate name:

BLACK ENGLISH
Standard Black English   ◄---------►   Black English Vernacular
         [SBE]   [BEV]

This paper focuses on the Black English Vernacular, since it is the home language in the Ann Arbor case, and the linguistic system the great majority of Black children bring to their first reading experiences. This vernacular is not known perfectly to six- or seven-year-olds; there is considerable language learning that continues into late adolescence (Labov et al., 1968). Further, more, there are many individuals in the Black community who are influenced by other dialects as they grow up. The most consistent vernacular is found among adolescents who are centrally located in their peer groups (Labov, 1972, Ch. 7) or among adults who live and work within the Black community (Baugh, 1979). It is not always possible for teachers to recognize these differences in social and linguistic status, with the result that classroom observations are often blurred (Garvey & McFarlane, 1968).

In this discussion, I will present some of the features that distinguish BEV from intermediate forms. Even though studies show that inner-city teachers can assume that the majority of their Black students participate in the BEV linguistic and cultural system, and that their approach to reading is profoundly influenced by it, it is important that teachers recognize intermediate forms. I will also suggest a number of strategies for applying our knowledge of BEV to the teaching of reading: these will apply equally well to children who use BEV in its most consistent form and those whose system is shifted some distance towards classroom English.

Educators are often presented with stereotypic descriptions of BEV far-removed from linguistic systems used in everyday life. Media coverage of the Ann Arbor Black English case described BEV with examples never used by anyone anywhere, such as, "He am so big an cause he so, he think everybody do what him say" (*U.S. News & World Report*, 3/31/80, p. 64).[5] More often, educators are exposed to stereotypes that preserve only those forms of BEV that most differ from classroom English, eliminating all variation as the result of "borrowing" or "code-switching." This is sometimes a hold-over from the earlier days of controversy, when creolists were interested only in isolating those forms that resembled the Caribbean creoles. Sometimes these stereotypes are proffered by people who have never studied tape recordings of the language as it is spoken. But in any case, BEV is a full-fledged linguistic system, with the range of inherent variation that all such systems have. BEV has some obligatory rules where other dialects have optional rules, some variable rules where the others have obligatory ones, and some rules that don't exist in any other dialects.

Many educators have borrowed Robert L. Williams' term "Ebonics" to refer to both the linguistic and cultural systems particular to Black Americans. The term is not widely used by linguists, but discussions of Ebonics programs refer to many of the linguistic features presented at the Black English trial. There is considerable convergence between proponents of Ebonics and those who prefer the concepts Black English and Black English vernacular.

Finally a word must be said about the question of *language* vs. *dialect*. "Is BEV a separate language?" The answer is that linguistics does not make a technical distinction between languages and dialects; the difference is more political than linguistic. It is therefore factually correct to say that Black people have a language of their own. But if it appears that BEV is closer to classroom English than, say, Hawaiian creole English or Jamaican English, then I would prefer to say that BEV differs much more from regional dialects of the North than from Hawaiian creole English or Jamaican English, and in its tense and aspect system, is quite distinct from the dialects spoken by white Southerners.

2. The Tense and Aspect System of BEV

Much of the Ann Arbor Black English trial testimony made reference to the *aspect* system of BEV, and newspaper accounts have usually featured one example of habitual *be*, as in *She be sick*. This is the most prominent and the most frequent of the BEV aspects: Geneva Smitherman's texts of converstions with the Green Road children recorded seventeen examples of habitual *be*. Tito B. alone used the aspect eight times over the course of a short interview. His statement, *When it be raining, I be taking it to school* is a good example of the habitual *be*.

Habitual *be* is especially important because it does not exist in any other American dialect.[6] It also exemplifies the positive side of BEV grammar. Its survival in the classroom demonstrates better than any other aspect how BEV makes useful distinctions that aren't made as easily in classroom English. Tito B.'s sentence (1) cannot be accurately translated as (2), but requires the expanded version (3) to convey the same meaning in classroom style:

(1) They be hitting on peoples.
(2) They are hitting people.
(3) They go around hitting people all the time.

Of all linguistic categories, the concept of *aspect* is the hardest to understand, and linguists disagree more about aspect than anything else. The meaning of *tense* is easier to comprehend for it situates an event at a point in time. Aspect communicates the *shape* of the event in time: Did it happen all at once (punctual), at many separate times (iterative or habitual), or was it spread out in time (durative)? Was it just beginning (inceptive) or was it finished and done with (perfective)? These are not clear and distinct ideas, but rather (as the term "aspect" implies) they represent ways of looking at things. Aspect is seldom found in pure form; it is often combined with questions of causation (is the event relevant to the present?) and reality (was it really so?). Finally, it is often combined with tense, so that we speak of a "tense-aspect system." Given all these complications, it isn't surprising that there is so little agreement on the meaning of general English aspects. There are almost as many theories to explain the contrast of (4) and (5) as there are linguists to argue about them.

(4) They hit people.
(5) They have hit people.

Since there is so little agreement about this topic in other languages, we should avoid dogmatism about the meanings of BEV aspects.

Before considering the meanings, we should look at the forms that these meanings hang on. Aspect can be expressed by independent adverbs like *already* or *really*, but the grammatical system we are interested in depends on short, one-syllable words placed before the verb. They usually don't carry stress, and as will be shown, in BEV the tendency for unstressed words to wear down or even disappear in speech is even greater than in other dialects. This tendency is triggered by the reduction of a short vowel in these monosyllables (*is, was, had, will,* etc.) to the obscure shwa. This reduction does not occur if the vowel is long. It is no accident that the BEV tense and aspect system is built on three words with long vowels: *be, do,* and *go.* In building on these three root words, BEV makes use of a single ending, the one inflection that does not tend to disappear in spontaneous speech. In other dialects, these auxiliary words preceding the verb are often reduced to single consonants like the future *'ll,* the present *'s* or *'re,* the past perfect or conditional *'d* or the present perfect *'ve.* In BEV, these single consonants / l, s, z, r, d, v, / are more often missing than present. But final /n/ does not disappear entirely: if it is not heard as a consonant, it is heard as a nasal quality of the preceding vowel. The basic BEV aspect system is made up of six words:

be	do	go
been	done	gon'

Notice that although the vowel quality changes when we add the *-n,* it does not disappear even in fast speech.

The three root words carry the same basic meanings as other dialects of English. *Be* refers to existence, *do* to action, and *go* to movement. But in the auxiliary, they have become specialized: *be,* as we have seen, indicates a special kind of habitual or repeated state; *do* has lost its content, and is used to emphasize other actions or carry the negative particle *n't,* as in other dialects; and *go* takes on a sense of movement towards confrontation, as in the standard English *go and.*

When we add the *n,* a new set of meanings emerge that move the action away from from the immediate present. *Be + n* has developed a complex meaning in BEV unknown in any other dialect or language.[7]

(6) I *been* know your name.

(7) I *been* own that coat.

In psychological terms, the speaker in example (6) is saying that he or she first got to know the other person's name, and in example (7) that he or she got the coat a long time ago. Both speakers stress that their respective situations remain true right up to the present.

When *n* is added to *do,* the meaning is *perfective:* the event referred to is completely and recently done, or really and truly done:

(8) You don't have it 'cause you done used it in your younger age.

(9) I done forgot my hat! I done forgot my hat!

(Labov et al., 1968, p. 265)

The addition of *n* to *go* produces the future, as in many other dialects. In the following example, the contrast between *done* and *gone* is particularly clear.

(10) After you knock the guy down, he done got the works.

(11) You know he gon' try to sneak you.

(Labov et al., 1968, p. 265)

The richness of the BEV tense and aspect system is most clearly apparent when we look at combinations of these elements. To begin with, *be* is combined with *done* to yield *be done*, as in:

(12) I'll be done put–struck so many holes in him he'll wish he wouldna said it.

(Labov et al., 1968, p. 266)

This combination is normally translated as a future perfect, equivalent to *will have* (and is often preceded by *'ll*). But there are sentences where this translation cannot be made and where in fact there is no straightforward translation into other dialects:

(13) I'll be done killed that dude if he lays a hand on my child again.

(Baugh, 1979, p. 154)

What is the speaker's meaning ? The statement was made with utmost seriousness by a man who had just witnessed his son being manhandled by a swimming pool aide. Normally, the English future perfect is the future form of the present perfect: it refers to the relevance of some future event for something else to follow. This is true of (12): the effect of sticking so many holes in the other person is that he will regret what he did. But in (13), we see a true perfect: the *be done* is attached to the result of the event. Instead of translating (13) into the nonsensical,

(14) I will have killed that dude if he lays a hand on my child again.

we would have to translate the perfective sense as something like "I will really and truly have to kill. . . " In trying to understand the cognitive differences between BEV and other dialects, considerable attention must be given to sentences like (13) which have no direct translation.

It also must be stressed that *done* is combined with *been* in a variety of ways to express events that have been completely accomplished in the past and are separated from the present.

A final use of the *n* suffix is the most familiar: it is in the progressive aspect that BEV shares with all other dialects of English. Here the *n* is usually combined with a short vowel, and variably with various forms of the verb to *be*, including the invariant *be* meaning "habitual." The meaning of *He's workin'* as opposed to *he works* is the same as in other dialects: it is a "durative," referring to extended activity that is actually carried out, usually simultaneously with some other event. With the habitual *be* in *he be workin'*, the progressive is freed from association with any particualr time. BEV speakers rarely use the *-ing* and use *-in'* close to 100 percent of the time. The *-ing* appears primarily in writing and cannot be really considered a part of the vernacular language.

This symmetrical system of *do, be, go,* plus *n* is not all there is to the BEV tense and aspect system. The past tense -ed is firmly entrenched in the under-lying grammar, though it is so often deleted after consonants that some speakers have trouble identifying it on the printed page (see sec. 3). In the auxiliary *had*, the final *d* appears again as a past tense marker. It is acquired early and is often used as the past perfect marker, meaning as in standard En-glish, "occurred before the last event mentioned," and to denote other past tense meanings as well. In addition to *be*, there is an auxiliary *steady*, which is often combined with *be*:

(15) Them fools steady hustlin' everybody they see.
(16) Her mouth is steady runnin.'
(17) Ricky Bell be steady steppin' in them number nines.

(Baugh, 1980)

Though *be* refers to habitual action, *steady* refers to much more. Baugh de-fines its scope as covering actions that are "persistent, consistent and continu-ous." In other words, *steady* has a lawful character: whenever this event could take place, it did.

We should also note the alternative form of the future:

(18) I'm a do it.

This form is found only in BEV and apparently is a semantic equivalent of *gon'*. Fickett (1970) has argued that the *I'ma* form (which occurs only with the first person singular) is semantically distinct from *gon'* and it means "im-mediate future." The evidence is not all in on this: it is one of the many areas in the semantics of BEV that needs further work.

A near neighbor of these aspects is a special BEV use of *come* as in

(19) He come tellin' me I don't love my parents.

Spears (1980) demonstrates that this is a "camouflaged" modal. It often looks like the standard English *come*. But the BEV speaker can also say "He come comin . . ." or "He come goin' . . ." The camouflaged modal *come* is a member of the BEV grammatical system that signals moral indignation: "He had the nerve to present himself doing this."

There are many similarities between these BEV forms and grammatical forms found in other dialects, and in creoles of the Caribbean and the Paci-fic.[8] Most of the BEV meanings, however, are unique combinations of se-mantic elements. There is every reason to think that BEV, like all other living languages, continues to develop its resources and enrich the cognitive system of its speakers.

To sum up, we can present the special features of the BEV tense and as-pect system as:

be	"habitual," applied to events that are generally so
been	"remote present perfect," conditions that were so a long time ago, and are still so
done	"perfective," events that are completely and/or really so
be done	"future perfective," events in the future that are completely, really so
been done	"past perfective," events in the past that are accomplished and really so
steady	"persistently, consistently, and continuously so"
gon'	"future and less really so"

The organization and symmetry of this system should now be evident. With the exceptions of the invariant *be* and *gon'*, these are seldom heard in the classroom and rarely in the Black English of radio and television. Even in intimate vernacular settings, many of them are rare: it is only when highly particular contexts arise that they are needed and used. If the tense and aspect system of BEV doesn't appear in the speech and writing of the classroom, how can it affect reading? The answer to this question will be easier if we look first at other features of BEV that have a more obvious connection with reading.

3. English Inflections in BEV

So far, we have looked at the special BEV system of conveying grammatical meaning by invariant words placed before the verb. Now we will look at the other end: how does BEV use the system of modifying meaning by putting inflections—usually single consonants—at the ends of words?

We have already noticed that many final consonants tend to disappear in BEV speech. This happens not only in the auxiliary, but at the ends of all words. The variable process of consonant deletion as it affects words and grammatical endings (the plural, the possessive, the past tense) has been studied in some detail. BEV is often described as a series of absences; to most people it looks like an over-simplified language "without grammar." It is said that BEV has no plural, no past tense, and no possessive, and that these categories are foreign to Black children. But a careful examination reveals that this view is highly exaggerated.[9]

We can first observe that some English inflections are present *more* often in BEV than in other dialects. One of these is the plural. While standard English has no plural inflection in words like *deer, sheep,* and *fish*, the corresponding BEV plurals are regular *deers, sheeps* and *fishes*.[10] Another example is the absolute possessive, as in:

(20) This is mines.

BEV has generalized the possessive inflection found in *John's, yours* and *hers.*

The past tense category is also quite secure. BEV speakers use the strong verb forms *gave, told,* and *left,* in the same way as all other dialects. In fact, it is even more regular, since the historical present seems to be used less by BEV speakers than by others.

The problem with the past tense is related to regular verbs ending in *-ed,* where the signal of the past tense is confined to a single consonant, /t/ or /d/. This signal is sometimes present, sometimes absent. But we have ample evidence that it is firmly located in the underlying grammatical structure representing the linguistic knowledge of the speakers. First, it is always present more often than the /t/ or /d/ in consonant clusters that do not signal the past tense, like *fist* or *old.* Second. when *-ed* follows a /t/ or a /d/ as in *wanted,* and a vowel breaks up the cluster, the final *-ed* is always present. Third, the past tense *-ed* is dropped less often before a vowel, and more often in difficult consonantal combinations like *mixed batter.* Fourth, the *-ed* never occurs where it is not wanted: we never find the past tense used for the present, as in *He walked home these days.* For these and many other reasons, it is certain that present-day BEV has the grammatical suffix *-ed* and speakers have knowledge of it that they can draw on in reading standard English primers.

The rate of deletion may be so high, however, that BEV speakers may not recognize the *-ed* on the printed page as a carrier past tense of meaning. To determine the presence of this ability, we devised reading tests including such sentences as:

(21) Last month I read five books.
(22) When he passed by, he read the poster.

The task here is to transfer the past tense signal in the first half of the sentence to the unique homograph *read,* which demonstrates the form of the vowel, /riyd/ vs. /red/, whether the reader had the past tense in mind. For BEV speakers who had reached the fourth or fifth grade reading level, there was almost 100 percent success in transferring the past tense meaning from the adverb *last month*; but with the past tense *-ed* in *passed,* the results were not much better than chance (Labov, 1972, p. 30ff).

The case of the auxiliary and verb *to be* is parallel. The finite forms *is* and *are* are sometimes present in their full form, sometimes in contracted form, and sometimes entirely missing. There is now ample evidence indicating that in present-day BEV, the dropping of the copula is simply an extension of the contraction process found in other dialects and in BEV (Labov, 1972, Ch. 3). Here, too, the full verb forms are available and are freely used by BEV speakers; in fact, young children use more full forms than adults. It is the contracted forms, or single consonants fused with the preceding word, that can cause problems. Young children find it very hard to connect chains like these:

/ay aem/ ←→ /ay am/ ←→ /aym/ ←→ /ay/

Several investigators have found that children in the second grade lack the ability to analyze *I'm* into *I am*, though all the facts surrounding them would suggest that connection.[11] Many BEV speakers of this age will respond:

(23) −You're not George Baker!
    −Yes I'm am!

Finally we come to the class of English inflexions representing the maximum distance between BEV and classroom English. Although the third singular *-s* of *he works hard* is occasionally present in the speech and writing of BEV speakers, studies show that it is not present in the underlying linguistic knowledge that children bring to school. For each of the four points raised in the above discussion of *-ed*, the answers are the opposite for third singular *-s*. There is no general process of dropping final *-s* in other words. It does not appear more often after /s/ or /z/, when a vowel appears between the stem and the consonant. When third singular *-s* does appear, there is no effect on the surrounding consonants or vowels; there is not even a reverse effect. It often appears in the wrong context, from the point of view of classroom English, as in

(24) He can goes out.   (Labov et al., 1968, p. 166)

For these reasons and many others, we believe that the task of acquiring consistent use of third singular *-s* is harder for BEV speakers than is learning to use *-ed* consistently. Furthermore, the problem is harder for BEV speakers than for Spanish speakers. Though Spanish has no mark on the third singular, the notion of agreement between subject and verb is fundamental to Spanish grammar. In BEV, it is not simply third singular *-s* that is absent. The general machinery of number agreement between subject and verb is barely represented in the grammar. The irregular alterations *have/has, do/does* and *was/were* are represented in BEV by invariant *have, do* and *was*. It is only in the finite forms of the verb *to be* that we find some agreement between subject and verb.

We discussed the absolute form of the possessive as an example of a grammatical category that is fully represented, even over-represented, in BEV. The opposite is the case when the possessive *-s* relates two noun phrases. In the great majority of cases, the possessive *-s* is absent for BEV speakers, and demonstrates many of the traits of third singular *-s*. In some cases, the choice seems to be categorical: *whose book* is not heard and is very hard to reproduce in repetition tests.

Thus a portrait of BEV inflections can be drawn of three distinct situations: features entirely absent from the underlying grammar of BEV, features present in the grammar but variably deleted to a point hard to retrieve, and features that are generalized beyond the point of the standard language:

ABSENT	VARIABLE	GENERALIZED
subject-verb agreement: 3rd singular[s]	regular tense [ed]	regular plural[s]
possessive [s] : noun adjuncts	contracted copula [s] & [r]	possessive [s] : absolute form

4. Loss of Information at the Ends of Words

In most of the language families of the world, words gradually become worn away at their ends. There are many reasons for this. While a principle of least effort is certainly involved, it is also true that the distribution of information must also be taken into account. The first sound or letters of a word are the most useful in helping the listener determine the meaning of the word; the last few sounds or letters may be completely predictable. For example, if a one-syllable word begins *des*-, there is only one way to finish it: with a *k*. Even if the /k/ was not pronounced, the word would have to be *desk*.

This tendency to lose information at the ends of words may be encouraged by the fact that the ends of words do not carry as much information as the beginnings, but it is not limited to cases where the information is not needed. In the course of linguistic history, sound changes in languages like Chinese and French have produced thousands of homonyms, words that have exactly the same sound, though they were once quite different. For languages that carry their grammatical information in the form of single consonants at the ends of words, this leads to a great deal of unhappiness in the grammatical system. English has lost most of its inflections through this wearing away process.

The Black English vernacular loses information at the ends of words in a more extreme fashion than other dialects.[12] But those who grow up speaking BEV, like speakers of other dialects, have many indirect ways to learn about the shapes of words. They do not necessarily pick the form of the word they hear most often as the base of their mental dictionary. If they are exposed to older speakers who have an underlying knowledge of the form of a particular word that includes all of the sounds in the standard dictionary entry, they will sometimes pronounce these full forms, particularly when the next word begins with a vowel. In some cases, where a stop consonant is sandwiched between two *s's*, as in *wasps, tests,* or *desks*, the stop may never be pronounced. Still, the *t* in *tests* can be discovered if a *t* reappears in the word *testing*. When young children are first learning to read, they may not yet have put together all the bits of information they need to arrive at the final solution—the shape of the word in the grown-up dictionary. Just as some think that *I* has an extra sound /m/, they may also assume that *desk* has only three sounds, or that *old* has two or only one.

Because the tendency to delete final /r/, /l/, /t/, /d/, /v/, and other consonants is more extreme in BEV than in other dialects, the relation between the spelling forms and the spoken language can be much harder to figure out for children learning to read and write the standard language. The following list contains some of the words that can be heard the same way. Each word stands for a member of a class of words: all the words that rhyme with it.

(a) The deletion of final *t* or *d* can give:

in simple words:

cold = coal	mist = miss	tent = ten
field = feel	paste = pace	pant = pan
world = whirl	must = muss	wand = wan

in the regular past tense:

rolled = roll	missed = miss	fanned = fan
healed = heal	faced = face	penned = pen

in the past tense of irregular verbs:

told = toll	lost = loss	went = when
held = hell	bent = Ben	meant = men

with the general merger of /i/ & /e/ before /n/:

penned = pinned = pen = pin
send = sinned = sin

(b) The deletion of *l* and *r* can give:

with the Southern deletion of the glide after back vowels:

told = toll = tore = toe
sold = soul = sore = so

with the more common Northern pronunciation:

sore = Saul = saw
cord = called = cawed

and generally:

guard = God	tool=too
par =pa	jewel = Jew

with the tensing of /e/ before /l/:
     held = hell = hail
     sailed = sail = sell
with the monophthongization of /ay/:

wired = wide = why	wild = wowed = wow
fire = far = fa	piled = Powell = pow
mire = mar = ma	tiled = towel

The examples are not intended to suggest that all of these words are the same for all speakers of BEV. With the exception of a few cases (like *pen* and *pin*), identity is variable. But the frequency of deletion can be very high, and the experience of the learned does not yield enough information to keep these words apart.

The differences between the spoken and written form can cause problems at each step in the reading process. When the child reads a word correctly, the teacher may not recognize this success unless he or she can also recognize the equivalent sets of pronunciations outlined above. As early as 1965, these patterns were presented to the National College Teachers of English to illustrate some of the special problems confronting a speaker of BEV learning to read (Labov, 1967). It was then proposed that teachers who conduct oral reading practice begin to make clear distinctions between mistakes in reading and differences in pronunciation. Since that time, the principle has been widely accepted, but we do not know to what extent it has affected classroom practice.

It is now possible to put forward a more concrete program for reading curricula incorporating these special properties of BEV. A great deal of reading research is devoted to the fundamental problem of the acquisition of the alphabet. We are not only concerned here with the learning of the alphabetic principle, but also with its use as a general tool in decoding the printed page. In the Harlem study of 1965-1968, it was shown that many young people were effectively illiterate. Researchers found, for example, twelve-year-olds who scored at the first or second grand level on the Metropolitan Reading Test. Yet surprisingly enough, every one of them had mastered the alphabet. Early mastery of the alphabet was apparent in the patterns of reading mistakes on reading tests and standardized tests as well. When someone did not recognize a word, and had to guess, the guess almost always had the same first consonant as the printed form, and the same first vowel. But the rest of the guess showed no relation to the letters on the page. A typical example shows (25a) read as (25b):

(25) a. I sold my soul to the devil.

  b. I saw my sour to the deaf.

The sentence has not been read and understood. But in attempting to decode its meaning, the reader hasn't neglected the alphabet. The alphabet has been used for as long as it could be trusted: for the first several letters. The weak connection between the last letters on the page and the form of the word as it is perceived and grasped by the reader has led to this loss of confidence. The same pattern appears clearly when we analyze reading errors. For seventeen pre-adolescent youth in the Harlem study, ages ten through thirteen, we considered all those misread words whose pronunciation had some relation to the letters on the printed page. The number of letters read correctly in each position were:

	N	1st	2nd	3rd	4th	5th	6th	7th
		\multicolumn{7}{c}{Letters read correctly}					
3-letter words	11	8	4	6				
4-letter words	77	65	55	45	31			
5-letter words	46	45	30	34	25	24		
6-letter words	26	26	19	20	19	15	10	
7-letter words	11	11	10	9	10	10	8	3

The problem is not the mastery of the alphabet itself, but one of acquring the confidence to use it consistently. The weak correlation between the spelling forms on the printed page and the forms of the words as they are spoken has apparently led many Black youth to limit their use of the alphabet to the first few letters—or more accurately, to lose all confidence in the value of the alphabet for the last few letters.

Preliminary results of reading research by J. Baron point in the same direction. Eleven Black and eleven white children were matched for their ability to read regular words (34 correct out of 51). On exception words, Black children scored better, averaging 30.3 correct out of 51, than white children, who averaged 27.6. But on nonsense words, which require alphabetic skills, the results were reversed: 30.9 correct out of 51 for Blacks, as against 32.5 correct for whites. Other tests confirm the small but significant tendency of Black readers to use the alphabet less than whites. If we were to distinguish the use of the alphabet at the ends of words from its use at the beginnings of words, this difference might well be magnified.

Though there are many unanswered questions on how the structure of BEV interacts with the business of learning to read, there are a number of clear findings that can be applied to reading curricula. But before considering strategies for putting this knowledge to use, we should complete our look at the whole picture. It isn't hard to see how the sound patterns of BEV affect reading. But what about the more abstract semantics of section 1? Forms like *be done* and *been done* do not appear very often in the classroom—neither in writing nor in speech. Is there any way in which the BEV aspect system enters into the process of learning to read standard English? The next section will show that this underlying semantic system may not be as far away from the classroom as it first appears.

5. Ambiguities of Tense and Aspect

The child who comes to school speaking BEV meets classroom English in two main forms: the teacher's speech and the printed words on the page. We've looked at some evidence about the result of interaction with the second: the full forms of words are hard to decipher, even when there is reason to think that adult speakers of BEV have the same full forms. It is also hard for children who speak BEV to make use of the final consonants that represent inflections, even when there is reason to believe that their own underlying grammars include this information.

There is no hard evidence on children's ability to interpret the speech of the teacher. But there are many indications that some of the speech signals of classroom English will be missed, and no reason to believe that children who speak BEV will automatically understand and absorb the standard system of tense and aspect.

We have seen that BEV-speaking children do use contractions like *We'll* and *They're* and *They'd*. But contractions are less common in BEV than in white dialects since they alternate with zero forms as well as with full forms. Among young children, full forms are more common than among older children and, as we have noted, contractions are often misinterpreted as in *Yes I'm am*. The *'ve* in *I've* or *they've* is particularly rare, and there is strong reason to doubt that the underlying grammar has a *have* auxiliary in the present perfect.

It is not generally realized that the full forms of auxiliaries are widely used in BEV. Typical BEV forms are shown below as (a) rather than as (b), which represents forms more common in white dialects:

    (26) a. I had come over.
         b. I'd come over.
    (27) a. We will have succeeded . . .
         b. We'll have succeeded . . .
    (28) a. We have said it . . .
         b. We've said it . . .

The past perfect of (26a) is very common among young Black children, and the uncontracted form is normal in the most vernacular speech. The *will have* of (27a) is formal; but the informal shift is to the simple future or to the complex *be done*. (28a) is again formal. The informal alternate, however, is not (28b) but rather the past tense *We said it*. In a word, there are many contradictions that are common currency for white children but not for Black children.

This disparity results in multiple ambiguity in the contact situation. The BEV-speaking child's problem shows up in this input-output diagram:

Teacher's Production	Heard As	Interpreted As
They will be there → They'll be there		future
	They be there	habitual *be*
They would be there → They'd be there		conditional
They have been there → They've been there		present perfect
	They been there	remote present perfect
They had been there → They'd been there		past perfect

Here are two situations where the grammatical information of classroom English may be neutralized, and open to a three-way interpretation by the listener. The multiple ambiguities shown here are only some of the problems resulting from structural mismatch in the learning situation. It might be argued that context will usually make the teacher's intention less ambiguous. But this can be said for any part of language. We do not know how many misunderstandings are needed to produce cognitive confusion of a more permanent sort. Nonetheless, it is reasonable for the teacher to be aware of potential confusions and try to avoid them.

When the forms on the left are found on the printed page, the students' problems are much more evident. The contracted forms are hard for BEV readers to interpret and relate to their full forms or zero forms. The readers we are most concerned with interpret words one at a time—with some of the bizarre results exemplified by (25b) above. Any steps promoting the shift to reading meaningful sentences will be a major step forward in reading. Any mismatch on the printed page between the readers' grammatical knowledge and the letters to be read can only delay that process.

For all dialects, there are homonyms in speech that must be rendered unambiguous if they are going to be correctly connected to the printed page. To be helpful, teachers must know what words sound the same and what connections have to be made. Two other sets of homonyms in BEV illustrate the principle.

It was noted at the outset that BEV grammar does not rely on words with short, reducible vowels so much as on words with long vowels that never disappear. Two long nasal vowels do a great deal of work for BEV:

(a) long nasal *e*:

> They haven't = They ain't = They 'e'
> They aren't = They ain't = They 'e'
> They didn't = They ain't = They 'e'

Most people realize that *ain't* can correspond to standard *haven't, hasn't, amn't, isn't* and *aren't*. But few people realize that BEV can also use *ain't* where other dialects use *didn't*.

(b) long nasal *o*:

> They are going to = They gon' = They 'o'
> They do not = They don' = They 'o'
> They will not = They won' = They 'o'

Here we have two future forms and one present tense form, all expressed by the same vowel. Such drastic reductions can create problems in working out the relationship between the colloquial forms and the full forms of classroom English.

6. Five Strategies for Teaching Reading to Speakers of BEV

This last section will outline five strategies for bringing our knowledge of BEV grammar into the day-to-day teaching of reading. It is not intended as a series of suggestions of how to teach reading: that is the business of teachers and educators who know the full range of problems and practices involved. These principles are put forward as a means of making linguistic knowledge available to those who design reading curricula. My aim here is to put into practice the letter and spirit of the Ann Arbor Black English decision, so that knowledge of the Black English Vernacular can be taken into account in the teaching of reading.

Strategy 1: Recognize reading errors: Teachers should be ready to distinguish between mistakes in reading and features of pronunciation typical of BEV. This strategy rests on the fundamental principle put before the National College Teachers of English in 1965, that the teaching of reading should distinguish true reading errors from differences in the ways that words are pronounced. The underlying concept is generally recognized: that reading is a way of deriving meaning from the printed page. But discussions of the trial have focused far more attention on the way children speak or are allowed to speak in the classroom. Arguments about "Black English in the classroom" have little to do with the Ann Arbor decision, and distract from the main task at hand: helping children learn to read.

Oral reading is not used to the same extent in every classroom. When children do read aloud, however, corrections by the teacher have considerable impact: they affect both readers and listeners at the same time. Certainly teachers should know enough about the constants and variables of BEV pronunciation to be able to decide whether the reader has misunderstood the message on the printed page. Thus, in

(29) When I passed by, I read the posters.

we can use the pronunciation of *read* to draw such a conclusion, but not the pronunciation of *passed*, since the final /st/ cluster is variable. In

(30) He lost his tests and hers too.

we cannot tell from the presence or absence of the /t/ in *lost* or *tests* whether those words have been read correctly, since the first is variable and the second always absent in BEV pronunciation; but we can judge from the /s/ in *hers*, because *her* and *hers* are never confused in BEV.

It is generally agreed that success in reading is the critical first step in the acquisition of basic skills, and all programs must be weighed against this priority. If educators should decide that training in standard English pronunciation is an essential step in reading, that should be undertaken as a separate program. But the bulk of current research indicates that success in reading is not dependent on pronunciation. Practice in imitating the teacher's pronunciation will not necessarily add to children's underlying knowledge of the language, since it has been shown that such superposed dialects do not develop systematic knowledge. Strategies 4 and 5 below may be more effective in this respect.

Strategy 2: Pay attention to the ends of words: Evidence has been brought forward showing that the loss of information at the ends of words is a critical factor in the use of the alphabet by BEV speakers. Yet reading programs pay far more attention to the use of the alphabet for decoding letters at the beginnings of words. I have reviewed a number of phonics texts in current use, and found that the majority devote only a small fraction of their lesson plans to final consonants, and that only one gave roughly equal time to beginnings and ends of words.

This idea does not apply only to reading programs that rely heavily on phonics. No matter how the curriculum is designed, some means should be found to focus the BEV reader's attention on the *d* in *child* and the *ed* in *walked* at an early age. Some reading teachers avoid paying too much attention to the ends of words because of the danger of reading reversals: getting *saw* instead of *was*. It seems to me that this is usually a minor problem compared to the major difficulties documented in section 4 above, and it should not be allowed to dictate the fundamental strategies used in teaching of reading.

I have tried to show that the potential knowledge is often present. If the task of the educator is to build on that knowledge, the means must be found to make it available to the reading process. One such means is presented as Strategy 3.

Strategy 3: Introduce words in the most favorable contexts: The most common way to introduce a new word is in citation form: that is, in isolation, or at the end of a short presentative sentence:

(31) This is a *desk.*

This method has the advantage of focusing attention of the word, with full final stress, and minimizing confusion with other information. Yet for BEV speakers this is not the best way to introduce a word into the reading process. It has been shown that BEV differs from other dialects in that consonant cluster simplification is relatively high before pause, and lowest before a following vowel. For a speaker of BEV, the full form of the word will be recognized more fully in the context

(32) There is a *desk* in this room.

This principle applies most obviously to spoken interaction, as when an adult is introducing a word for the first time, or reading a new lesson, or even correcting a mis-reading. But we have reason to think that it also affects individual and silent reading in the course of the complex feedback between decoding, recognition, and encoding.

This is one case where differences between dialects are most relevant to teaching strategies. For some white dialects, like that found in Philadelphia, consonant clusters are preserved most often in final position. In these cases citation form of instruction works very well. But for other dialects (New York City, BEV, Puerto Rican English) final position behaves like a following consonant. Here, a following vowel helps bring out the form of the word more clearly.

Adopting this strategy would not favor Black children at the expense of the others. For every speaker of English, final consonants are pronounced far more often before a following vowel than before the next word that begins with a consonant, and the advantage of final position is, at best, not very large.

Strategy 4: Use the full forms of words: This principle follows from all that has been said about the role of contracted forms in BEV. Contractions are not alien to BEV and are frequently used in speech. But for many young speakers of BEV, they are not easily analyzed as distinct from the word they are attached to, or related to the verb phrase. It would therefore be best to avoid the use of such contractions in reading texts and in the first steps of learning to read. Some textbook writers would interpret this alteration as a step backward, since they feel that

(33) This is Rex. He is my dog.

is stiff and traditional. They would tend to replace it with the more relaxed and colloquial

(34) This is Rex. He's my dog.

Although this second form is less stilted, it does not automatically help speakers of BEV. For them, the first form is likely to be more clear and natural. A more extreme kind of problem is created by

(35) This is Rex. He's my brother's dog.

which introduces the possessive 's sandwiched between two noun phrases, and is especially hard for BEV speakers to recognize and use. It might be easier for them to apprehend

(36) The name of this dog is Rex. He is my brother's.

which does not involve any letters that are hard to recognize.

The choice of sentence forms is not based on difficulty in understanding the basic message. BEV speakers will not necessarily misunderstand *He's my brother's dog.* But it will not be easy for them to interpret the two 's signals. If they ignore them, it will be one more step towards the loss of confidence in the alphabet we have already witnessed.

It might be argued that sooner or later all children must learn to read sentences like (34) and (35). This is certainly so. But the strategies suggested here are designed to facilitate the first steps in reading and to avoid any conflict of BEV and classroom English. The next strategy looks toward further reading steps and toward bridging the distances between linguistic systems.

Strategy 5: Relate full forms to contracted forms: Here we enter an area that goes beyond the first steps in the teaching of reading. The central principle involved is to make use of the child's own knowledge of language by developing the relation between the various forms that he or she uses in everyday speech, especially those that are closest to classroom English. Thus the relation between full, contracted and deleted forms of the copula:

(37) a. He is on my side of the room.
      b. He's on my side of the room.
      c. He on my side of the room.

is implicit in the child's production of language but not necessarily available to him for further advances in reading. One of the most extreme examples of such expansion and contraction is found in the English periphrastic future, where the child's competence may include such forms as:

(38) a. I am going to do it.
      b. I'm going to do it.
      c. I'm goin' to do it.
      d. I'm gonna do it.
      e. I'm gon' do it.
      f. I'm 'on' do it.
      g. I'm 'o' do it.
      h. I'm a do it.

The child may recognize the relationship between any two of these. But faced with the contrast between (38a) and (38g) or (38h), most people will not see much relationship at all.

There are many ways in which this relationship can be developed within the reading program or in the more general teaching of English. At each step, specific linguistic information is needed, and this information has to be made available to those curriculum designers who are prepared to use it. Even if linguists were better at communicating their own knowledge of grammar to other scholars and to the general public, their suggestions alone are likely to be wide of the mark. This communication is submitted to educators as part of one effort to put our linguistic knowledge to use in the critical problem of improving the teaching of reading to American children.

NOTES

1. The analysis of Black English presented here rests on the work of many other people besides my own. The research in New York City was a joint effort, and I am greatly indebted to my colleagues Paul Cohen, Clarence Robins and John Lewis at every stage of field work and analysis. The work of Walt Wolfram and Ralph Fasold forms an essential part of our present knowledge of Black English, though I have not provided all the references identifying their contributions. My debt to John Baugh, John Rickford, and other scholars from the Black community appears throughout: the most creative work of the last decade comes from participant-observers who have drawn upon their entire social experience to solve linguistic problems. Finally, I must acknowledge my debt to Beryl Bailey, William Stewart and Joey Dillard, who never stopped insisting on the importance of parallels between Black English and the creoles of the Caribbean, until even the most backward members of the linguistic community were at last convinced, including myself.

2. Because the Judge's preliminary intructions to the plaintiffs seemed to convey a very narrow notion of linguistic description, the plaintiffs did not include in their presentation the problem of barriers caused by differences in the use of language: the area named

by Hymes the "ethnography of communication." It is likely that cultural and linguistic conflicts contribute not only to educational failure, but also to behavioral differences in areas such as ways of showing attention, of turn-taking, and of showing respect and deference to adults.

3. Only one educational program was presented by the plaintiffs to show how knowledge of Black language and culture could be used in reading programs: BRIDGE, written by Gary Simpkins, Grace Holt and Charlotte Simkins, and published by Houghton Mifflin. Simpkins testified on the cognitive difficulties of Black youth who had to translate the standard English semantic system into their own framework as well as decode the alphabet. BRIDGE avoids this problem by a smooth transition between tapes and reading texts in BEV, an intermediate form, and standard English. The content draws on Black culture and folklore throughout. BRIDGE is written for adolescent youth who are returning to the problem of learning to read, while the focus in the Ann Arbor Black English case was more on younger children in their first approach to reading. The same general problems, however, are addressed in both.

4. Research in the 1960's was concentrated primarily among Black youth in the inner cities, and it is their use of BEV that is reported. Baugh's research in Pacoima, California (1979) demonstrated that adults who lived and worked in the Black community used exactly the same linguistic system in peer group and family contexts.

5. One exception to this was the series of newspaper stories generated by Geneva Smitherman in Detroit before the trial. These included accurate descriptions of the BEV tense and aspect system.

6. Rickford (1974) shows how the *doz be* forms of Gullah shift gradually to the invariant *be*, with the same "habitual meaning," responding to the overt stigmatization of the *doz*. He considers an alternative origin in the Anglo-Irish *does be*, but rejects this since Anglo- Irish dialects do not generally delete the first word.

7. The *been* with this meaning is always stressed and shows a low-pitch accent. Rickford (1975) reports a series of experiments showing dramatic differences in the interpretation of the sentence "She *been* married." 92 precent of his Black subjects answered "yes" to the question, "Is she still married?" and only 32 percent of the whites.

8. The perfective particle *done* is also used by white speakers throughout the Southern states. It remains to be   shown whether the semantics of their use is the same as the semantics of the BEV *done*. The combination *be done* is not used by white speakers.

9. The plural [s] suffix is often absent from "nouns of measure" when they are preceded by a number: *three cent, five year*, and so on. This is not peculiar to BEV: many other dialects show more systematic use of this feature, such as the north of England dialect of Leeds.

10. Jane Torrey (1972) found this in her research among second graders in Harlem.

11. William Stewart (1968) pointed this our in an early article and Torrey's work in

Harlem found experimental confirmation.

12. The wearing away of inflections is a slow evolutionary process in most languages, but in the formation of pidgins and creoles it is much faster. The long history of BEV seems to be dominated by the reverse of this evolution, as inflections are replaced under the influence of the standard language. But the existence of this long-term decreolization does not end the normal process of wearing away in rapid and spontaneous speech. Grammatical particles like [ed] that have been replaced are still frequently deleted—even more drastically than in other dialects, since the earlier tradition without [ed] is not entirely eliminated from the scene.

REFERENCES

Bailey, Beryl. *Jamican creole syntax*. London: Cambridge University Press, 1965.
Baugh, John. Linguistic style-shifting in Black English. Ph.D dissertaion. University of Pennsylvania, 1979.
———. Steady: Progressive aspect in Black English. Mimeographed, 1980.
Deutsch, Martin, Katz, Irwin & Jensen, Arthur. *Social class, race and psychological development. New York: Holt, Rinehart* & Winston, 1968.
Dillard, J.L. *Black English*. New York: Random House, 1972.
Fickett, Joan. *Aspects of morphemics, syntax and semology of an inner-city dialect*. West Rush, N.Y.: Meadowbrook Publications, 1970.
Garvey, Catherine & McFarlane, Paul T. A preliminary study of standard English speech patterns in the Baltimore city public schools. *Report No. 16* Johns Hopkins University, 1968.
Jensen, Arthur. How much can we boost IQ and scholastic achievement? *Harvard Educational Review*, 1969, *39*.
Joiner, Charles W. Memorandum opinion and order in Civil Action 7-71861, *Martin Luther King Junior Elementary School Children, et al. vs. Ann Arbor School District Board*, July 12, 1979.
Labov, William. Some sources of reading problems for speakers of non-standard Negro English. In A. Frazier (Ed.), *New directions in elementary English.* Champaign, Illinois: National College Teachers of English, 1967.
———. *Language in the inner city*. Philadelphia: University of Pennsylvania Press, 1972.
Labov, William & Robins, Clarence. A note on the relation of peer-group status to reading failure in urban ghettos. *Teachers College Record*, 1969, *70* (5).
Labov, William, Cohen, P., Robins, C. & Lewis, J. A study of the non-standard English of Negro and Puerto Rican Speakers in New York City. *Cooperative Research Report 3288. 2 vols.* Philadelphia: U.S. Regional Survey, 1968.
Rickford, John. The insights of the mesolect. In D. DeCamp & I. Hancock (Eds.), *Pidgins and creoles: Current trends and prospects.* Washington, D.C.: Georgetown University Press, 1974.
———. Carrying a new wave into syntax: The case of Black English *been*. In R. Fasold & R. Shuy (Eds.), *Analyzing variation in language. Washington, D.C.:* Georgetown University Press, 1975.
Spears, Arthur. Come: a modal-like form in Black English. Paper read at the Winter meeting of the Linguistic Society of America, Los Angeles, 1980.

Stewart, William. Continuity and change in American Negro dialects. *The Florida FL porter*, 1968, *6*, 14-16, 18, 304.

Torrey, Jane. *The language of Black children in the early grades.* New London: Connecticuit College, 1972. [ERIC ED 067 690]

Turner, Lorenzo. *Africanisms in the Gullah dialect.* Chicago: University of Chicago Press, 1949.

SOCIAL PERCEPTION: THE *KING* DECISION
;E-RELATED LITIGATION

Ronald C. Woods

Mr. Woods is Director of the Afro-American Studies Program at Eastern Michigan University and Adjunct Lecturer of Law at the Center for Afroamerican and African Studies at The
University of Michigan. His children attend the Ann Arbor Public Schools but were not
plaintiffs in the *King* case.

Mr. Woods offered the following remarks as a participant in a panel discus-
sion on media and public responses to the King *case. Panelists were asked to*
respond to two questions: "What do you see as the most important issues in
meeting the educational needs of students who speak vernacular English in
public schools?" and "What do you believe are the understandings and misun-
derstandings of the issues in the press and by the public?" As a member of the
Ann Arbor community and a parent of children attending Martin Luther
King, Junior Elementary School, Woods viewed at close range the attitudes
and events surrounding the litigation of the King *case. Much of what he says*
is related not only to the situation in Ann Arbor, but also to problems na-
tional in scope.

I. ISSUES IN MEETING THE EDUCATIONAL NEEDS OF STUDENTS WHO SPEAK VERNACULAR ENGLISH

The basic issues as I see them are three: attitudes, quality of knowledge,
and instructional methods. How constructive and realistic are the attitudes
held about students who are speakers of vernacular English? What is the quality of knowledge about the setting in which speech patterns are acquired? Will
the instructional methods used result in language and reading proficiency for
the students involved? I will first deal with the problem of attitudes.

Teachers' Attitudes Toward Vernacular English Speakers

It is important that a teacher have a positive yet realistic perception of a
child's ability to learn. Few, if any of us, would disagree with this. What many
more of us need to appreciate is that there is a tendency, ranging from weak
to strong, to view vernacular English speakers as less intellectually capable

than their mainstream speaking or code-switching counterparts. This tendency is reflected in numerous subtle and not so subtle ways and can have a devastating though unintended impact on the child. It is a tendency born of class, ethnic and racial biases that are integral parts of Western society's view of the world. Among its several consequences is the likelihood that the teacher, miscalculating the student's intellectual ability, will not address the problem with the techniques required. There is also the danger that the child's creative and analytical capacities may not be challenged to their outer limits nor given free rein to develop and that the self-fulfilling prophecy of expectations of low achievement will materialize. Over the long run, the intangible factor of attitude will result in quite tangible deficiencies in the student's arsenal of skills.

Teachers are obviously not immune to the elitism, racism or ethnocentrism in American culture. Yet, by virtue of their frontline involvement at key stages of a child's development, teachers bear heavy, some would say unfair, responsibilities in this area. Meeting that responsibility begins with recognizing how these forces operate and with committing oneself to resist the inclination to negatively characterize vernacular English speakers. It requires a willingness to be painfully introspective. It is a difficult but imperative task.

Students' Attitudes Toward Themselves

Attitudes flowing from elitist or ethnocentric cultural norms have an equally damaging impact upon the student's self-perception. Judge Joiner's comments in the *King* case are pertinent here. In offering an explanation of why the plaintiff children read poorly, even though their teachers had tried many instructional methods, he stated, "In the process of attempting to teach students how to speak standard English, the students are made somehow to feel inferior and are turned off from the reading process."

The gravamen of this statement is attitude. What teacher attitudes are directly or indirectly conveyed to the student? And how is the student's attitude toward self affected? The fact of the matter is that little will succeed in meeting the educational needs of vernacular English speakers unless these children sense that others believe in their capacity to achieve. As the Ann Arbor decision made clear, the student's image of his or her intellectual ability affects the acquisition of basic skills. Poor self-image hinders aggressiveness in the formal pursuit of learning, inquisitiveness about social and physical phenomena, and the attempt to situate oneself in the total human experience.

I end this portion of my remarks with a comment on how the teacher attitude/student perception issue manifests itself where Black teachers are concerned. Does the Black teacher tend to be more effective than the white in instructing Black students, and if so, why? Judge Joiner alluded to evidence that Black teachers in pre-*Brown** segregated settings seemed to fare better than their contemporary white counterparts in teaching reading to students who spoke Black vernacular. Marva Collins, a Black teacher at the Westside Preparatory School in Chicago has recently been acclaimed for her success in teaching Black students to read without resort to the steps called for in *King.* Similarly, many Black adults with backgrounds similar to those of the plaintiff students point approvingly to the demanding, non-conciliatory regimen set by their own Black former instructors.

It is not clear precisely how sharing the same racial heritage with a teacher operates in a student's education. One interpretation suggests that any success which the Black teacher does achieve is partly due to attitudes shaped by his or her own life experiences. According to this view, the Black teacher tends to have a more sound grasp of the Black child's social and cultural environment than the white teacher. He or she is therefore less likely to see vernacular speech as a badge of ignorance and is more prone to recognize the importance, to the student and to the larger Black society, of cultivating the student's latent potential. Having a greater stake in the issue, the Black teacher may adopt an approach which, though "no nonsense," reflects empathy and a more positive orientation.

The teacher's race and success in training the vernacular speaker cannot be exactly correlated. Too few vernacular speakers are proficient in language arts to support such a contention. Yet commonality of race between teacher and pupil is a variable still awaiting thorough analysis by researchers and program developers. If not directly addressed in the *King* case, this matter is within the web of issues raised. It will continue to inject itself into any worthwhile dialogue on the education of the vernacular English speaker.

Attitude of School Community Toward
Vernacular English-Speaking Students

The collective attitude of the school community—students, teachers, administrators, staff persons, parents and other residents—is an important feature of the total picture. Even when vernacular English speakers and their teachers hold constructive attitudes, the likelihood of educational success is lessened if the broad community is either misinformed, intolerant of vernacular English issues, or unsupportive of the instructional remedies being employed. Community attitudes may range from informed understanding to pa-

---

* *Brown v. Board of Education of Topeka*—for further discussion of this case see chapter 1, page 3. [Ed.]

ternalism to racial or class animosity. I will limit my comments to the stigma-tizing which may result from the more negative attitudes.

The process of stigmatizing may well precede any formal recognition by teachers, students or parents. As early as the kindergarten level, students have already begun their socialization to the elitist, sexist, ethnocentric and racist biases that are in turn conveyed to their peers. These biases have clearly be-come operative if vernacular speakers are categorized according to where they live, how they behave, their style of dress, their type of food, their academic performance, their manner of fighting, and so on. These attitudes may foster a counterproductive isolation of vernacular English speakers, lead them to adopt defensive coping mechanisms and breed cleavages within the student community. The dangers are greatest where economic divisions are distinct (as is the case in the Martin Luther King, Jr. Elementary School setting) and where competing social perceptions are present.

All parties must be careful not to indulge cultural arrogance, whether around the dinner table or in the classroom, and not to nurture the creation of a caste system in the student population. The needs of vernacular English speakers can only be met in an atmosphere where challenges have been met and prejudices minimized.

Parents' Attitudes Toward Their Children

Last, I will touch briefly on the attitudes of parents of vernacular English speakers toward their children. Like most parents, these parents are intensely concerned with their children's proficiency in language arts and have faith in their children's capacity to achieve. And they are pained when the process does not produce the desired results. Yet, positive parental attitudes may be ineffectual unless they assume a functional role in the learning process. In ful-filling that role two points should be taken into account.

The first is the need to be aware that the quality and frequency of a child's exposure to literature, conversation, and other non-classroom educa-tional stimuli affects the level of proficiency acquired by the child. This pro-position has particular bearing where the vernacular speaker in concerned.

On the other hand, the classroom forum is limited in its ability to insure that each child is maximally educated. Class size, teacher morale and budget restraints are among the limiting factors. The plight of the functional illiter-ate demonstrates how a child can be short-changed by systematic limitations within the public schools. No parent is safe in assuming that the child is be-ing educated merely because that child is attending school and is not other-wise being singled out as a problem.

On the other hand, the educational system, by and large, responds most positively to the white, the articulate, the attractive and those viewed as representative of the cultural mainstream. Those who do not meet these characteristics, e.g., the vernacular English speaker, will be engaged in a struggle throughout their educational careers to force a greater degree of responsiveness to their learning needs. Recognizing these dynamics and aggressively seeking non-classroom educational experiences will aid in countering the otherwise inevitable ill effects.

The second point is to realize that exposure to extra-curricular stimuli need not necessarily be a function of race or class. The white middle class does not have a corner on providing its children non-classroom educational experiences, nor should it be permitted to. Although affluence clearly facilitates access to educational opportunities outside of school, it is not a prerequisite to them. For the economically marginal or the impoverished, part of the challenge is to see the community and the world as a laboratory and to be resourceful in search of what the public and private domains have to offer. It is also a challenge to establish an atmosphere that will encourage the student to be an active seeker rather than a passive recipient of information. It is a challenge to inculcate in the child a sense that he or she can make a difference in the quality of life in this world. Only at this juncture does parental attitude assume its catalytic potential.

Quality of Knowledge

The second major topic I would like to explore is the quality of existing knowledge about the environment within which speech patterns are acquired. This issue is important for two reasons. First, attitude, though not always rationally formed, is largely shaped by our understanding of history and by our perception of the prevailing social and economic order. Our knowledge of race, class, and ethnicity—factors which often set apart the vernacular speaker—is heavily laden with misconceptions and parochial perspectives. The result is that Americans too often view their society as they wish it were rather than as it is. Skewed visions of history result in skewed attitudinal approaches to vernacular English speakers. Second, a more accurate sense of the acculturation process undergone by Blacks in the United States, of the relationship between American and African cultural patterns, and of the environmental features that promote or inhibit learning would further the search for teaching techniques in the area of vernacular English.

Instructional Methods

The last major issue I would like to comment on is the search for instructional methods designed to help students bridge the gap between vernacular and mainstream English. As a lay person in the fields of linguistics and reading, I can neither make an expert critique of the plan being implemented in Ann Arbor, nor propose a slate of specifics for any other. But I can offer the following suggestions which I believe should be taken into consideration in any plan to address the vernacular question.

1. Techniques should draw upon the most recent social science and historical research available.

2. Any adopted plan should seek to develop in teachers informed and constructive attitudes about race, class, and ethnicity. In one sense, the teacher must have a firm informational foundation upon which fair evaluation of students' performance can be based.In another, the teacher's attitude helps determine not only whether vernacular speakers will learn to read, but how they will feel about themselves once the process is completed.

3. Where feasible, efforts should be made to involve the parents in the instructional process. Parental assistance in creating pertinent non-classroom educational experiences is vital. Where evidence exists that a relatively passive approach to this is taken at home, the school should initiate consultations designed to promote greater activism in providing educational stimuli.

The court's ultimate concern , and properly so, was that the students learn to read. The plaintiffs in this case were seeking to prevent another generation of functional illiterates from falling through the seams of the educational system. We ought to be mindful that, by and large, the children with whom we are concerned are representatives of the groups that have historically borne the brunt of this country's development and that have been and remain marginal in this society. This is a matter of some concern for those of us who are Black, Hispanic, or Appalachian. These children are part of the vital core that will provide to their respective groups the intellectual and technical leadership upon which their group's empowerment will be based. Lurking in the wings is a necessary reordering of American society in which all stand to benefit. It is this larger picture that we should keep in mind as we grope for answers to these questions.

II. UNDERSTANDINGS AND MISUNDERSTANDINGS
IN THE PRESS AND BY THE PUBLIC

I will now consider how the Ann Arbor Black English decision is being perceived by the public and portrayed by the press. The public's misunderstanding of the case and the broader questions it presents will be my major concern here. I will begin with comments on the shape the issue has taken in Ann Arbor. The bulk of my attention, though, will be on the national Black community's perceptions.

The Ann Arbor community's grasp of the issue can more accurately be described in terms of agreement/disagreement than in terms of understanding/misunderstanding. After the community had had a couple of days to read its newspapers, assess the coverage by the local and national electronic media, listen to spokespersons and talk about the issue, there emerged a general comprehension of the basic aspects of the court's ruling. It was generally agreed that the school's efforts, though involving a variety of materials and methods, did not culminate in reading achievement for the plaintiff children, that the school's failure to take Black English into account in teaching students to read was a causal factor, that the inability to read was an impediment to equal participation in instructional programs, and that the School District Board was obligated to take appropriate action to help teachers identify Black English speech patterns and to use that knowledge to teach vernacular speakers to read standard English.

There was thus a shared sense of what the decision held, but a divergence of opinion about what it meant. Public debate over the implementation and implications of the case began almost immediately and has continued up to this moment. A host of issues, described below, were generated by the ruling.

First, aside from the educational policy endorsed by the court, was the decision legally sound? How could Judge Joiner state that the teachers may have contributed to the students' failure to learn by not taking into account the Black English language system, yet also find that "each teacher (had) made every effort and used the varied resources of the school system to try to teach the students to learn to read?" Could one reconcile the court's contention that the students were made to feel inferior with its finding that there was "no direct evidence" that teachers treated the home language as inferior? Further, while holding that Black vernacular did not constitute a barrier *per se*, the court did speak of the probable negative consequences of attitudinal barriers to the plaintiff children's learning. As a legal proposition, was the Judge correct in finding the School Board liable and in basing claims for legal redress upon speculative assessments about the role of attitude, particularly in the absence of evidence of discrimination?

Second, in the interest of clarifying the legal and educational issues, did not the District have an obligation to appeal the decision through at least one step of the appellate process?* Would allowing the decision to stand unchallenged not be an unwarranted smear on the teachers' and on the Districts' educational reputation? Or was it time to bury the legal hatchet, recognize the

_____

* The Ann Arbor School Board initially voted to appeal the case. However, in an emotionally charged meeting one week later, the Board decided by a one vote margin not to appeal.

pedagogical and social merit of the decision, and attend to the business of education?

Third, should the plans implemented at Martin Luther King, Jr. Elementary School be extended to all other schools where Black vernacular English speakers were in attendance? Or should such a decision await an evaluation of the program and some determination of whether it was needed elsewhere? Despite the court's invitation to the School Board to draw a plan embracing other elementary schools, the plan has not been extended beyond the Martin Luther King, Jr. Elementary School staff.

Fourth, what of the motivation of the Ann Arbor Public Schools in the planning of this very conference? Some have maintained that the conference is premature since no assessment of the inservice program has yet been made. Some see it as an attempt to capitalize on the notoriety which has come to the District by virtue of a lawsuit which it adamantly opposed. Some have questioned the apparent exclusion from conference participation of principal persons or key supporters in the plaintiff's case. Still others have objected to the conference being held a mere week prior to the District's School Board election—an election upon which, at least according to the *Ann Arbor News*, the future of racial balance in the city's public schools may hinge. The District administration responded that the conference's purpose was neither to evaluate Ann Arbor's successes and failures, nor to retry the case, but to explore the many dimensions of the vernacular English issue. It has also been pointed out that, at the invitation of the National Institute of Education, mutual planning began several months ago and did not contemplate the upcoming election.[*]

Finally, to what extent have the parties utilized the press to their benefit? In a case such as *King v. Ann Arbor*, the opinion of the public may ultimately be as important as that of the court. While the efforts of both sides to disseminate information has been commendable, neither seems to have abandoned the adversarial posture. The result has been that each bit of information has too often been treated as an evidentiary finding for the public's consumption. This approach is not optimally conducive to the flow of objective information that should take place in every community. One would hope that the dialogue informing the community would reflect the highest standards of accuracy.

The Ann Arbor Black English controversy offers materials for a rich case

[*] The Board election one week later saw a "liberal" majority of one replaced with a "conservative" majority of one. No definitive analysis has yet been made of what relationship exists between the election results and the Black dialect question.

study of a community struggling to remedy the consequences of this nation's racial history. The issue involves not only the cultural debate over content and pedagogy in the educational process; it also causes us to reflect upon the historically evolved economic, political and spatial relationship of Blacks to whites. Because communities are unique, it would be risky to extrapolate from the Ann Arbor experience general propositions about how any particular community faced with a vernacular English conroversy may respond. I do not attempt it here. But I do suggest that the following variables should be taken into account by researchers and analysts:

1. *The Community's Literary Level and Reading Habits*: Some measure of the prevalence of reading difficulties related to vernacular speech can be garnered from determining this. The community's reading habits should provide some indication of that community's desire to know about a vernacular controversy and its willingness to take the time to find out. While a high literacy level or sound reading habits may not eliminate differences of opinion about the vernacular question, it should at least lessen ignorance or gross misunderstanding about it.

2. *The Philosophical Orientation and Relative Power of the School Administration, School Board and School Staff*: How receptive each of these units is to the challenges posed by the vernacular question will shape the direction in which a community moves. In speculating on these entities' degree of responsiveness, conventional labels such as " liberal" and "conservative" have only limited utility. The hybrid alliances that will increasingly mark school district politics defy such tidy packaging. Rather, one should seek a factually derived assessment of where each unit, and the individuals within it, stands on specific racial/educational matters. That unit's grasp of the subtleties and intricacies of systemic racism must be weighed. Equally important is the relative real power of each division of school district governance to translate its persuasions into district policy.

3. *Access to, Control Over, or Philosophical Concurrence with the Media*: A major item is whether individual constituencies have the means to communicate their position on any phase of a vernacular English issue to the larger community. Does each group have access to a credible news organ to disseminate its point of view? This question recognizes the centrality of the media's role in forming public perceptions. It takes into account the circumstances which, in an actual or *de facto* sense, give visibility to a particular line of thinking. Again, we are confronted with the matter of power relationships, this time in terms of media access, control, or usage.

The Perception Held by the National Black Community

The final portion of my remarks survey the national Black community's response. As I suggested earlier, the future of Blacks in the United States depends heavily on reversing the trend of functional illiteracy that has siphoned off too much of the race's creative potential. The Black community's perception of the vernacular English controversy will shape policy at the local, state, and national levels. I will begin by describing the Black community's perception of the Ann Arbor Black English decision. I will then advance an interpretation of that perception from the perspective of Afro-American history in general, and *Brown v. Board of Education of Topeka* in particular.

"Judge Rules in Favor of Black English." This headline typifies media coverage of *King v. Ann Arbor.* It said everything. It said nothing. Did it mean that the judge had found Black English to be a legitimate means of instruction and oral and written expression in the schools? Or did it mean that the court had found Black English to be a language system that had to be taken into account in formulating instructional methods to train vernacular speakers to become competent readers of mainstream English. That the latter description was correct could sometimes be discovered by reading the fine print, sometimes not. Despite lengthy news analyses and the circulation of copies of the official opinion, the belief that the court had ordered the teaching of Black English took hold in some quarters and has been slow to die.

Within the national Black community, the reaction has been diverse. One segment has applauded the ruling as a long-fought-for social and legal recognition that African cultural norms are present in the contemporary speech patterns of African descendants in the United States. Another segment, more pragmatic in its orientation, has not seen it as a comment on African heritage, but rather as a decision to meet the Black dialect speaker where he or she is and to offer a practical approach to the acquisition of reading skills. Still a third segment, for a myriad of reasons, has viewed the decision quite negatively. This last group exhibits not only a fair difference of opinion on the Black English question, but confusion and misunderstanding as well. For these reasons, it merits further examination. This group, which numbers several prominent individuals and organizations, contends that the Ann Arbor decision is a liberal capitulation to questionable social science theory and a backward step in the struggle against illiteracy. Both the Detroit chapter of the NAACP and the national NAACP, for example, have taken the ruling to task as a retreat from equal educational opportunity. Journalist Carl Rowan has stated his belief that Judge Joiner, though well-intentioned, is doing Blacks a disservice by providing Black youth crutches that will retard their acquisition of skills.

Some members of the National Urban League also oppose the decision. In the organization's *State of Black America Report, 1980,* a publication that includes government and corporate entities among its readership, Dr. Bernard Watson, Vice President for Academic Administration at Temple University offers the following assessment:

". . . This case . . . gives further support to the stereotypical beliefs that black students' learning must be treated as remedial."

"Here we go again: another way is found to prove that black youngsters can't learn as well as other students. The psychological and sociological mumbo-jumbo directed at black students continues . . . Students find another excuse for not buckling down to the difficult but important task of learning their native language which will enable them to move through the academic maze . . ."

"It is time . . . for black Americans to be reminded that employment tests, and others best known by initials such as SAT's ACT's, MCAT's, LSAT's and GRE's are screening devices which act as barriers and keep many blacks out of colleges, under and unemployed, and out of graduate and professional schools. All of these screening devices utilize standard English, not black English."

(It is not clear whether Dr. Watson's comments represent the official position of the National Urban League. In a syndicated column, Vernon Jordan, president of that organization, views the decision as a positive step in equipping teachers to better understand vernacular English speakers.)

How does one analyze the thinking typified by these responses? I suggest three possibilities, no one of which is applicable to all critics of the decision.

The first is that some members of this group have either received inaccurate or incomplete information or have been rather careless in their reading of the case and the available literature. In that case there is little commentary to offer.

The second possibility is that opposition stems from a firm belief that the decision smacks of paternalism and has enormous potential for abuse. According to this view, the ruling gives racists a legitimate cover for their belief in the lack of intellectual capacity among Blacks. In addition, it allows for a more lax approach to the development of skills at a time when rigor is essential. For this group, the rebuttal that the Ann Arbor case is concerned precisely with the acquisition of standard reading and English skills is only so much theory that will evaporate as compassion breeds a less than demanding learning climate and lower expectations for the Black child. The accomodating teacher will unwittingly become an accomplice to a second-rate education. What is needed, this school of thought contends, is more Marva Collinses who will frontally challenge Black students to learn. For critics who fall into this second category, the likelihood is small that they will be convinced to abandon their position by anything other than substantial improvements in the plaintiff children's reading skills. Yet, even such evidence as this may not be convincing to persons concerned with the spread of counterproductive paternalism in educational settings.

I suggest that a third source of criticism is the historical ambivalence which many Blacks feel toward Africa and toward manifestations of blackness contrary to Western cultural standards. A brief look at how this cultural dilemma reveals itself in the vernacular English controversy is helpful.

Eight decades ago, W.E.B. Dubois graphically depicted the dilemma in his classic, *The Souls of Black Folk* (1903). He wrote:

> ". . . It is a peculiar sensation, this double consciousness, this sense . . . of measuring one's soul by the tape of a world that looks on in amused contempt and pity. One ever feels his twoness, —an American, a Negro; two souls, two thoughts, two unreconciled strivings; two warring ideals in one body. . . "   (p. 16-17)

> " . . . The history of the American Negro is the history of . . . this longing . . . to merge his double self into a better and truer self . . . He would not Africanize America . . . He would not bleach his Negro soul in a flood of white Americanism . . ."   (p. 17)

> " . . .(the) seeking to satisfy two unreconciled ideals, has wrought sad havoc with ten thousand thousand people, . . . and at times has even seemed about to make them ashamed of themselves"   (p. 18)

Over the generations, this spiritual tension has been reflected in the persistence of two major variants of Black social theory. Integrationist philosophy, to which many Black English critics subscribe, is one of the key strands. This philosophy has premised Black progress upon the incorporation of Blacks into all facets of American society. It has encouraged interracial cooperation in achieving this aim and has called into question few assumptions about the political, economic or cultural organization of life in the United States.

Nationalist thought is the other variant. It has based social advancement upon altering the power balance in the American social order more favorably toward Blacks. It has typically eschewed coalition politics and has relied upon race-centered politics, institutions and arrangements to facilitate this change in power relationships. Nationalism has represented a greater challenge to the political,cultural and at times, economic foundations of the American experience. Of the two strands of thought, integrationism has received more favorable treatment than nationalism from the American intelligentsia and technocracy. Many Americans view integrationism as the only legitimate Black social philosophy. Yet integrationism, and its precursor assimilationism, have always vied with nationalist thought for the allegiance of Blacks. The controversy can be traced through the nineteenth century from the Frederick Douglas/Martin Delany debates, to the controversy in the 1920's between the NAACP and the followers of Marcus Garvey, to the more current discussion about the feasibility of an independent Black political thrust.

What is more important for our purpose is each philosophy's orientation toward Africa. On the cultural plane, the nationalist faction has, by and large, maintained a stronger identification with Africa. It has adopted a more positive approach to African cultural legacies and encouraged social patterns resistant to the American acculturation process. Within the integrationist perspective, however, such characteristics have been perceived as slowing the pace of assimilation and have, therefore, been viewed less tolerantly. For those of this persuasion (and I do not here include all integrationists) the historical or cultural legacy of Africa has either been down-played or denigrated: witness Belle's rather prejorative treatment of Kunta Kinte's efforts to retain his cultural moorings in the television adaptation of Alex Haley's *Roots*. To many Blacks, Black English is a disturbing manifestation of the African or Afro-American heritage. It is seen as an aspect of lower-class Black life that merely emphasizes the cultural distance between preferred American standards and those operating in sectors of the Black community. For Blacks of this mindset, it would be heresy to admit that any function is fulfilled by this language, let alone an educational one.

This reaction, however, is not unique to this issue nor to this time. It tends to surface wherever questions of Blackness or African origins offer challenges to perceived Western norms. More often than not, it reduces the issue to an absurdity. It leads to illogical analyses and to an inability to examine the issues for their worth. Thus, the cultural moribundity that a decade or more ago allowed some detractors of Black studies to reduce it to "Soul Food 101" today prevents a thorough consideration of the pedagogical and cultural merits of the Black English decision. The same mentality hinders an open look at American cultural dynamics and the vast implications for Western culture inherent in a more politically viable Afro-American and African population. This group of integrationists may well be conceptually incapable of approaching the issue constructively, save with a rigorous amount of self-examination, or with a strong appeal to its pragmatic, results-oriented instincts. The Duboisian dilemma continues.

There is an irony here that may be overlooked by those who fear this decision will slow the pace of assimilation. Afro-Americans of nationalist leanings may choose to see the Ann Arbor decision as an affirmation of African survivals or as a recognition by American courts of the importance of incorporating a nationalist perception of social reality into educational theory. (This is true to a degree but it is doubtful that many educators, jurists or the broader public recognize it.) Nonetheless, *King v. Ann Arbor,* as a legal opinion, is an extremely integrationist statement. It calls for the ultimate acceptance and internalization of mainstream English. In the process, a Black vernacular language system will be pushed to the periphery if not eliminated all together. The ultimate contribution of Black vernacular, as articulated in this decision, is a methodological one, i.e., to assist the search for new, effective approaches to reading instruction. On the basis of this case, one cannot say, however, that Black vernacular has made substantive inroads into the *corpus* of American language or that it has otherwise been legitimized. In this sense, the Ann Arbor decision embraces predominant features of the integrationist/assimilationist ethic. In effect, a nationalist perspective is used to achieve integrationist aims. If this were better understood by those in the integrationist wing who dissent from this decision, their acceptance of the case would likely be greater.

The case thus stands as a challenge to the national Black community to reject that which is sterile in the integrationist conception of culture, to examine the Black group acculturation experience, to develop and articulate a social perception of race and ethnic group relationships in this country, and to translate that social perception into curriculum. The body of knowledge from which the content of American education is drawn, still awaits an infusion of new methodologies and new substance—an infusion which neither mainstream American scholarship nor its ideological adherents can provide. The Black intelligentsia must therefore recognize the potential created by the Black English decision and must seek to enhance its capacity to chart the course for developments in the Black vernacular field. Failing this, *King v. Ann Arbor* may represent not only the first, but the furthest penetration of a non-integrationist social perspective into educational practice.

Finally, I want to discuss this case in light of *Brown v. Board of Education of Topeka*. I suggest that the Ann Arbor decision in certain respects should be located in a continuum of cases that originate with *Brown*, and that understanding and acceptance of the *King* decision by the national Black community and the larger population will be enhanced if it is so viewed.

There are two considerations here. First, basic to both cases is the concept of equal educational opportunity. In their quest for equality, *Brown* and much of its progeny, focus much more attention on the logistics of dismantling unconstitutionally segregated school systems through pupil reassignment, busing and the like. However, *King v. Ann Arbor*, as did the earlier *Milliken v. Bradley* (II), shifts the focus to the pedagogical and curricular components of equal educational opportunity. Whether the shift portends the reemergence of "separate but equal," whether it results from a more vigorous non-integrationist sector of Black educators, or whether it is a seasoned response to the lessons of a quarter-century of desegregation efforts, it seems likely that the classroom setting will continue as a focal point of activity in this quest.

Second, both *Brown* and *King v. Ann Arbor* concern the intangible effects of this country's racial history. The former focuses on the damage done to the child's self-perception caused by the practice of segregation. The latter treats the harm to the child's self-esteem and to his or her acquisition of skills caused by even unintended negative assessments of the child's home language. The Ann Arbor decision recognized that ethnocentrism and racism pervade all phases of the educational process in this country. It is a reminder that the race question has many dimensions and that, if not insoluble, it may yet be the most challenging issue facing society.

It is proper that in future discussions about educating vernacular speakers we consider the public's understanding. That understanding plays an integral role in making the educator's task easy or difficult. The search for this understanding will be far advanced if the public is willing to be informed, willing to examine the philosophical foundation of its reactions, and willing to recognize the continuum between the Ann Arbor decision and its precursors.

LANGUAGE VARIATION IN AMERICAN ENGLISH VERNACULARS

John Baugh

Dr. Baugh is an Assistant Professor of Linguistics and Anthropology at the University of Texas at Austin. He is currently at the Center for Applied Linguistics in Washington, D.C. on a Ford Foundation Post Doctoral Fellowship. His current research interests include both bilingual and bidialectal phenomena from the standpoint of production, perception, and corresponding linguistic attitudes.

In order to fully utilize our human resources in the future we must a-chieve some objective understanding of the social and cultural differences among various groups in American society. As Hall and Freedle (1975) have indicated, "melting pot" theories have been misleading. Linguistic science and history can be used to delineate the actual subgroupings of this peculiarly American melange. I will borrow from these fields to examine three American English vernaculars: Black vernacular English (BEV), Hawaiian Pidgin English (HPE), and American sign language (ASL).* Unlike many American ethnic di-alects with (verbal) bilingual traditions, the preceding vernaculars have e-merged at greater social distance from standard American English (SAE). This background of isolation complements the linguistic differences found in our modern classrooms.

The fact that Black children have reading problems has been known for quite some time. Although the available linguistic evidence suggests a correla-tion between Black children's reading proficiency and their use of Black En-glish, it is difficult to convert these findings into practical educational guide-lines. We can begin to approach the problem by looking at some common so-cial denominators among users of BEV, HPE, and ASL and by viewing these social factors within their proper historical context. Each history can be examined from the standpoint of the speech community members and the re-search of scholars who have studied these communities. For example, there are significant similarities regarding the birth and subsequent research on both

* Dorothy Lee has made some helpful suggestions regarding ASL. Her reseach in this area has been quite valuable to me. I am, however, solely responsible for statements about deaf people made in this paper.

BEV and HPE: both involve a pidgin (i.e., contact vernacular) genesis with en-suing decreolization in the direction of SAE. More directly related to dialect differences with SAE, these newer dialects were born as a result of New World trade. Most other ethnic minorities in the United States can identify their an-cestry with well-established European languages possessing rich literary tradi-tions. BEV and HPE, on the other hand, are spoken vernaculars with deep oral histories. Storytellers are still very popular and are often held in high esteem in these vernacular communities. Although it may have been possible, quite some time ago, to equate speech community membership with ethnic and/or racial boundaries, the increasing social stratification of American minorities—to all sectors of society—no longer allows us to link ancestry with speech in any hard and fast way. Our evolution has given rise to states of linguistic di-versity, a particularly critical fact where reading skills are involved.

The case for American sign language differs somewhat. First of all, the minority is distinguished by a biological handicap rather than by racial or eth-nic heritage. Several early studies of the relationship between ASL and signed English suggested that we had another "Diglossic" situation developing. Re-cent studies, however indicate that where there are significant syntactic dif-ferences between ASL and signed English, we may be closer to a bilingual sit-uation.

Many language-based problems are best expressed by members of the mi-nority groups themselves. The following quotation from a thirty-two year-old male BEV consultant outlines some of the major problems shared by all of these vernacular speaker /signers. His observations about minority limitations serve as the foundation for my discussion.

> ". . . I feel like nothing . . . that no one should be limited. This is some-thing that I feel pretty close to about limits anyway. I feel like Black per-sons has enough limits on them now . . . and humans as a whole has—has limits. So, Black music, or Black awareness should be geared in the direc-tion of Blacks, let me say, first, and then spread all over. Because when Blacks become aware of themselves it's gonna be spread anyway."

It is instructive to associate these limitations with social and linguistic pheno-mena. The first part of this discussion will review purely linguistic differences. Examples will be provided pin-pointing sources of confusion when acquisition of SAE is the primary objective. I will then turn again to some of the relevant social issues and compare them to other ethnic groups with bilingual histories.

Let us begin by considering some of the linguistic characteristics of BEV. For the sake of illustration, Table 1 contains several non-standard features of BEV and examples of their SAE equivalents.

Table 1: Nonstandard Features of Black English Vernacular English and Their Approximate SAE Equivalents

form	BEV	SAE Approximation
be (habitual)	They be tellin' 'em the same thing. All the homeboys be hustlin'.	They're always telling them the same thing. All of the boys are always hustling.
been (stressed)	I been had that car. She been bought that record.	I've had that car for quite a while. She bought that record long ago.
multiple negation	They ain't not brothers can't make no track team. It ain't no way they ain't gon go.	There aren't any brothers that cannot make any track team. There is no way (that) they are not going to go.
be done (future)	They'll be done drunk up all the beer. I'll be done got my own C.B. waitin' on him.	They will have already finished drinking all of the beer. I'll already have my own C.B. if I wait for him (to buy it.)
steady (aspectual)	They be steady rappin'. You just be steady on everybody's case.	They are constantly rapping in a persistent way. You are just on everyone's case in a constant and persistent manner.

SAE-to-BEV copula variation (is ﹥ s ﹥ $\emptyset$) or (are ﹥ re ﹥ $\emptyset$)

 He is coming → He's coming → He coming.
 We are leaving → We're leaving → We leaving.

The grammatical forms illustrated in Table 1 accord with the linguistic rules of BEV. In some cases, as in the absence of the copula (i.e., *is* or *are*), we can readily identify the equivalent SAE sentence. For example, "He coming" is clearly the BEV counterpart to the SAE "He's coming" or "He is coming." In other cases, like that with BEV *steady*, there is no corresponding SAE substitution.

These differences can be explained historically. There has been a long and often heated debate regarding the history of Afro-American dialects. This discussion has reflected changing attitudes within the general population as well as the intensification of research on minority groups in general. The most current historical analyses suggest that BEV has been influenced by a complex pattern of African and English sources. In the past these influences were characterized by the "creole" and "transformational" hypotheses.

The histories of English vernaculars are quite pertinent to pedagogical issues. Since our modern dialects emerged out of the complexities of American history, many BEV speakers employ non-standard sentences, like those in Table 1, in grammatically productive ways. These linguistic facts alone, to say nothing of other social impediments to education, can represent critical conceptual hurdles for these BEV students. It is therefore difficult to design educational programs sensitive to the ethnic or physiological backrounds of BEV and other minority students. To dwell on the differences between BEV and SAE, however, could be misleading. As Labov has observed, the similarities between BEV and SAE are often difficult for speakers to detect with specificity in ordinary conversation (Labov, 1972).

To further illustrate the point we can turn to the variable nature of past tense marking in HPE. The following passage was produced by a native adolescent Hawaiian among his peers. The discussion focuses on the speaker's aunt and how she became paralyzed in a confrontation with other native Hawaiians:

"Auntie Mary was picking up the chili peppers, eh . . . My auntie Mary was picking up chili peppers, eh? So . . . she . . . the guys was . . . see, get this . . . They was in the house it just like, uh, patio—like had screen, eh? So my auntie an' them was sleeping inside there. They was, they—so my auntie Mary *wen go* outside was gon pick chili peppers at the tree. [Night time?] Yeah. Cause, so she started picking 'em and then from on top they stay on the mountain and she [unintelligible]. So thing was coming down, so my auntie, my auntie told us that . . . so my auntie was . . . they was calling her for get away from there, eh? But she couldn't hear already because, you know, the guys was singing . . . and the pounding and all that. And the guys *wen come* and they *wen stop*. All my auntie an' them could do was just, you know, . . . watch. So the guys came and they get the bull, eh? . . . in the front. [Their leader?] Yeah, so my auntie Mary just look at 'em. So the bull, you know, the leader, look back and *wen go* they was talkin' in Hawaiian, eh? If the lady in front of them get family inside the line—and she never have, eh? So the guys *wen go*, you know, pick her up and slam her down and was doing all kind stuff. And, she wasn't like that. You know I no joke you too; after her whole right . . . her whole right side was paralyze(d), eh? I never know that 'til my auntie just told us that. I thought she just *wen got* into a car accident and she *wen die* after that."

The preceding passage is quite useful here, not so much for the exposition of HPE, but for the fact that it reveals multiple locations of variation with SAE. In Table 2A, some of the 'wen + Vb' sentences are presented with their SAE equivalents. Table 2B examines additional SAE options along with their HPE counterparts.

Table 2a: Past Tense Options in Hawaiian Pidgin English

A	B
...so my auntie Mary *wen go* outside was gon pick chili peppers.	...so my auntie Mary *went* outside was gon pick chili peppers.
And the guys *wen come* and they *wen stop*.	And the guys *came* and they *stopped*.
...so the guys *wen go*, you know, pick her up and slam her down...	...so the guys, you know, *picked* her up and slam her down...

Table 2b: Potential Sites for HPE Nonstandard Variation

A	B
...they *wen call* her for get away from there.	they *was* calling her for get away from there.
Auntie Mary *wen go* pick up the chili peppers.	Auntie Mary was picking up the chili peppers.
So my auntie (n) them *wen go* sleep inside there.	So my auntie (n) them *was* sleeping inside there.

In nearly every case we find that the *wen* form can be used optionally to mark past tense. The nature of this variation is far more complicated than my brief remarks suggest, but for pedagogical purposes we can recognize that the separate vocabulary item *wen* does the same grammatical work as do /-t/ and /-d/. Furthermore, these morphological endings are very difficult to hear in ordinary conversation due to their phonological brevity. The nature of the HPE variation is not strictly governed by internal linguistic processes and therefore provides additional stylistic options not contained within prescriptive SAE norms. As with Black English, the similarities between HPE and SAE present a greater source of confusion to students than when there is a clear difference between the dialects.

Before turning to sign language we must again appreciate an important socio-historical fact: Black speech and HPE have been isolated from SAE for predominantly geographic reasons. Deaf ASL signers, on the other hand, are not delineated along recognizable social boundaries. Nevertheless, there is a common trait of isolation from SAE.

To best illustrate ASL speakers' traditional isolation from SAE, cases where substantial linguistic differences exist will be considered. The use of the word "glass" in SAE is a good example of different lexical (i.e., vocabulary) requirements. Speakers of English, regardless of dialect, will appreciate that the same word, "glass," can be used in the following sentences:

1. The *glasses* are filled with iced tea.
2. I need some new reading *glasses.*
3. Windows are made of *glass.*

Each of the preceding sentences clearly refers to different types of glass. The special problems deaf people would have if they employed a single sign (i.e., a single lexical entry for ASL) to refer to different types of "glass" should be apparent. In ASL this difficulty has been resolved by introducing new lexical items. In other words, ASL will employ different respective signs to refer to "drinking glasses," "eye glasses," or "windows." Whereas spoken SAE may use a single vocabulary item, ASL requires three separate "signs." This lexical expansion is highly productive because it eliminates the possibility of a single ambiguous referential term.

Another linguistic gap between ASL and SAE rests on grammatical grounds. Sentences 1 through 4 are examples of (nearly) equivalent sentences for ASL, BEV, SAE, and HPE respectively:

1. ASL   Touch finish California you? (accompanied by raised eyebrows to convey a question)
2. BEV   (Have) You (ever) been to California?
3. SAE   Have you ever been to California?
4. HPE   You ever stay in California?

ASL has a significantly different syntactic structure where *you* appears in clause final position. The complementary facial expression is also important to reinforce the question status of the sentence. One could argue that we are looking at structural differences in both vocabulary and grammar common to bilingual communities. At the very least, ASL clearly reflects a greater degree of syntactic difference from SAE than do BEV and HPE. In the latter two cases there is a good degree of grammatical similarity to SAE.

One final illustration (Table 3) emphasizes some basic neurological differences related to the channel of communication unique to ASL (see Hymes, 1974).

Table 3: Production and Reception Differences for Speech and Sign

	Means of Production	Means of Perception
Sign	Hand Articulation	Visual Reception
Speech	Vocal Articulation	Auditory Reception

Linguistic errors further reinforce the physiological differences between ASL and spoken language. With speech we find that "spoonerisms" or "slips of the tongue" usually occur in environments where communication demands a high degree of articulatory dexterity. ASL signers encounter similar phenomena in "finger fumblers," or statements that require awkward hand-movements.

There is an unquestionable "feeding and bleeding" relationship between the emergence of socially stigmatized dialects and the social isolation of speech community members from the dominant dialect. In all of the illustrated cases, folk beliefs among the general populace apparently reinforced existing dialect boundaries. Until recently, for example, members of the speaking community often regarded non-hearers as mentally deficient. Attempts have been made to correct this false impression such as the establishment of communication programs offering training in ASL. Nevertheless, in order to appreciate the pressures on sign language, we need to recognize the relationship between dialect variation and the historical circumstances that fostered these linguistic differences.

Practitioners in the past placed overwhelming emphasis on teaching the deaf to speak; many continue to do so today. It is preferable, they argue, to integrate deaf people into the speaking population instead of isolating them from it. Because the speaking majority is unlikely to learn ASL, the signing minority has been encouraged, and in some cases coerced, to adopt speech. The argument behind this position is largely social. It presumes that the motivated deaf child is willing to make personal sacrifices in order to communicate with members of the speaking population. Others, primarily among the non-hearing population, have claimed that they would rather use ASL with fluency among a restricted population than communicate less effectively with the larger speech community.

Social pressure has marred attempts to debate the issue on an equal footing. Constant pressure, including occasional corporal punishment (e.g., slapping the hands of ASL signers), has been used to eliminate ASL in favor of SAE. This pressure has given rise to the belief among some members of the deaf community that ASL is an inferior form of communication. This attitude of inferiority is historically consistent with the BEV and HPE situations as well. Native speakers/ASL signers have been made to feel that their primary dialect/language is flawed in some substantive way. This belief is, again, the result of cultural stereotypes and has no basis in linguistic fact. The social pressure to use SAE created an atmosphere where native vernacular speakers/signers came to adopt two or more styles of speech/sign.

The linguistic factors affecting HPE and BEV are, once again, similar to the socially isolating circumstances faced by signers. The social origins of HPE and BEV, however, have more in common with one another than with ASL.

Thus, with the possible exception of ASL, the emergence of these contact vernaculars differs from the typical histories shared by most ethnic groups in the United States.

Native Hawaiians and Africans imported to the American continents as slaves faced the special problem of adopting a linguistic system at complete variance with their own. Moreover, they were forced to adopt these languages from positions of social subordination. Just as it remains unlikely that the speaking majority will adopt sign language, the traditional stigma associated with BEV and HPE tended to reinforce linguistic boundaries through racial and social rejection. To fully appreciate why contemporary children are still having reading problems we must consider the unique linguistic history of slavery in the United States.

To circumvent possible uprisings, slave-traders regularly separated Africans who spoke the same language. Slaves were forced to learn a completely different language without benefit of formal education. This practice represents one of the first documented cases of language-planning. Three factors are central to this unique history:

1. *Isolation from Native Languages*: By preventing the use of the native language, reliance was forced on the new language—in this case, English.

2. *Acquisition of Existing Non-standard English*: For the most part, slaves learned (non-standard) English from two sources: fellow slaves or white overseers. These sources of influence account for various features of BEV traceable to African sources in some instances, and non-standard white southern influence in others. It should be noted that these overseers were often members of the lowest social strata of the white population. Since the overseer's dialect was one of the first models of English for the slaves, their speech reinforced their subordinate status.

3. *Illegality of Reading Instruction*: This was perhaps the most devastating restriction of all because slaves were denied access to traditional literary tools explaining the grammatical rules of SAE. This legacy, along with the oral traditions of African peoples, gave rise to a strong oral tradition among Blacks throughout the Americas. Educational institutions, until recently, have not been sensitive to the sociolinguistic history of BEV speakers.

At this point I would like to suggest that the vernaculars discussed in this paper present different pedagogical problems than do the more obvious cases of bilingualism. Einar Haugen (1972) has examined the problem of English vernaculars among several minorities in the United States. He has observed that a standard dialect is characterized by a minimum range of linguistic variation but maximum social utility. The difficulties associated with becoming bi-dialectal, he argues, are most clearly revealed when socialization is taken into account. One must acquire, in addition to linguistic skill, the ability to deter-mine the dialect appropriate to various social situations. Haugen's discussion of bilingual competence clarifies both similarities and differences for bidia-lectal competence: "The key to the bilingual's competence lies in the necessi-ty for alternating his codes, a process usually referred to as switching." (p. 314). The key to bidialectal competence thus appears to lie more with a perceived need for *alternating styles*, and this process can be referred to as *shifting*.

Comparing two well-known cases in the United States, Figure 1 represents the degree of linguistic overlap between standard Spanish/standard English and BEV/SAE.

Figure 1
Common Linguistic Denominators for Standard Spanish/Standard English and BVE/SE

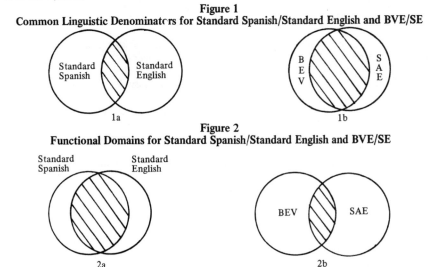

1a   1b

Figure 2
Functional Domains for Standard Spanish/Standard English and BVE/SE

2a   2b

The points of intersection between Spanish and English are comprised largely of shared vocabulary. It is therefore unlikely that intelligible conversation would take place between monolinguals, at least without the help of major translation. In the phonological, morphological, lexical, and syntactic BEV/ SAE situation, there are far more similarities than differences. The larger shaded area in Figure 1B indicates this greater range of shared linguistic fea-tures. Logically, these shared linguistic systems should provide greater mutual intelligibility during conversation, especially since their dialects are similar. What distinguishes the vernaculars, in short, are their differing language func-tions.

In figure 2 the ven diagrams correspond to the functional domain of each of the represented language/dialects. The inversion of the shaded area reveals the fact that BEV and SAE, while structurally similar, are used for very different social purposes. Standard Spanish and standard English, meanwhile, are both well-established written languages which can be used, as Haugen suggests, with maximum social utility. Therefore, while BEV and SAE share many linguistic characteristics, the functional differences—not the linguistic —appear to perpetuate the separation of these closely related dialects.

By recognizing cultural, social, and linguistic differences in the proper historical contexts, we will be better equipped to provide students with equitable educations. Hopefully, our efforts today will provide tomorrow's student with greater opportunities to be productive within the mainstream society with a greater chance of success.

BIBLIOGRAPHY

Baugh, John. The politics of Black power handshakes. *Natural History*, October, 1978.

Bickerton, Derek. On the nature of a creole continuum. *Language*, 1973, *49*, 640-69.

Fasold, R.W. & Wolfram, W. Some linguistic features of Negro dialect. In R.W. Fasold and R. Shuy (Eds.) *Teaching standard English in the inner city*. Washington, D.C.: Center for Applied Linguistics, 1970.

Frishberg, Nancy. Arbitrariness and iconicity: Historical change in American Sign Language. *Language*, 1975, *51*: 696-719.

Hall, W.S. & Freedle, R.O. *Culture and language: The Black American experience*. Washington, D.C.: Hemisphere Publishing Corp., 1975.

Haugen, Einer. *The Ecology of Language*. Stanford, California: Stanford University Press, 1972.

Hymes, Dell. *Foundations in sociolinguistics*. Philadelphia: University of Pennsylvania Press, 1974.

Labov, William. *Language in the Inner City: Studies in the Black English Vernacular*. Philadelphia: University of Pennsylvania Press, 1972.

Rickford, John. Carrying a new wave into syntax: The case of Black English *been*. In R. Fasold and R. Shuy (Eds.), *Analyzing variation in language*. Washington, D.C.: Georgetown University Press, 1975.

Stewart, William. Toward a history of Negro dialect. In Frederick Williams (Ed.), *Language and Poverty*. Chicago: Markham, 1970.

Wolfram, Walt. *A sociolinguistic description of Detroit Negro speech*. Arlington, Virginia: Center for Appled Linguistics, 1969.

———. The relationship of white Southern speech to vernacular Black English. *Language*, 1974, *50*: 498-527.

MID-SOUTH ENGLISH, MIDWESTERN TEACHERS, AND MIDDLE-OF-THE-ROAD TEXTBOOKS

Gary N. Underwood

Dr. Underwood is an Associate Professor and Director of English for Foreign Students in the Department of English at the University of Texas at Austin. His research interests include language variation, language attitudes, American English, Australian English and English language instruction. Dr. Underwood has served for four years as Assistant Editor of the *Linguistic Atlas of the Upper Midwest.*

Most adult Americans are accustomed to associating certain variations in English with particular regions of the country. A stranger does not have to say too much before we decide that he or she must be from New York, Virginia, New England, Texas, or somewhere else. Almost always these impressions of someone's "accent" of "brogue" are based upon features of pronunciation so that when we hear a speaker pronounce *park* as [pak] we assume he or she is from Eastern New England. Likewise *law* pronounced as [loᵊ] suggests New York City, *about* pronounced as [ə b ʌ ot] suggests Eastern Virginia, *Colorado* pronounced as [kɑlərédo] suggests western Texas, and *Nevada* pronounced as [nəvædə] suggests the Rocky Mountains region. Our responses to such "accents" can be either intellectual or emotional. Rationally, we may acknowledge that such differences are purely relative functions of place, just as we know and expect Englishmen, Australians, South Africans, and Americans to all sound different from each other. Despite our informed consciousness of linguistic relativity, we may also respond subjectively to these differences, our emotional reactions reflecting those attitudes we hold toward people who, within our experience, speak with those particular accents.[1]

Negative subjective reactions to language differences are an unfortunate fact of life. The stereotypes and biases that accompany them impair healthy interpersonal relationships. Unfortunately, exposure to facts and reason alone does little, if anything, to change a person's attitude toward language differences.[2] Thus, regardless of how hard we try in teacher training curricula to impart to our students such concepts as linguistic relativity and regardless of what lengths we go to to expose them to different varieties of American English, we are foolish to expect their intellectual growth to be accompanied by a lessening of linguistic prejudice. The teacher-trainees may acquire a veneer of linguistic sophistication; their stated values may change radically, but their attitudes, like cockroaches which have been sprayed with the exterminator's pesticide, are likely to persist unscathed. All people are victims of their language attitudes, but the Pygmalion effect is a special concern for us teachers since our attitudes toward the varieties of English spoken by our students affect, consciously or subconsciously, our evaluation of student performance.[3]

Regional differences in American English are not merely confined to "accent." They extend to vocabulary, such as the Texan's expression *soda water* for what Michiganders call *pop*, and into morphology, as in the Southerner's ubiquitous *you-all* (pronounced [yɑl] in Texas) for the second person plural pronoun. Less well-known is the fact that regional differences also exist in the realm of syntax, or the ways we arrange words into patterns to form sentences.

Purely regional variations, that is, those with distribution patterns which do not correlate with such social variables as sex, education, social class, or urbanity of the user, carry no social stigma in their native region, where attention, either intellectual or emotional, is rarely called to them. Normally they become the topic of comment in only two situations: when they are noticed as distinct from other regional variants or when they are compared to some real or imaginary supraregional monolithic standard. Even then, such comparisons rarely degrade the regional variants in the minds of their users.

Of particular interest is what happens when regional variants—perfectly respected in their home territories—are transported into other regions. How those migratory variants will fare in the new community may depend in large part on the status of their users in this new setting. This paper will examine how language of the Mid-South (Kentucky, Tennessee, Arkansas, and southern Missouri) has been carried northward by working-class whites who have migrated to cities such as Detroit, Ypsilanti, Pontiac or Flint to work in the automobile plants. Since these people are similar educationally, occupationally, residentially, and culturally, they form a fairly homogeneous minority in these Michigan communities. Consequently, a good many features of English which have been respectable variants in the Mid-South have become socially marked in Michigan.

In Michigan, the "accents" of those with linguistic roots in the Mid-South certainly draw attention to themselves, and Michiganders of a different linguistic and cultural tradition respond to those "accents" in predictable ways. While Mid-South "accents" have the power to affect virtually any kind of social interaction, syntactic features of Mid-South English are potentially more significant than "accents" in Michigan classrooms. (In the past, speaking English with a Mid-South "accent" was sufficient cause for being placed in speech therapy classes in some Detroit-area schools. Hopefully, more enlightened policies now prevail.[4]) Even though people may respond strongly to different characteristics of pronunciation, it is generally recognized that in the United States differences of grammar provoke far stonger judgements about a speaker's intelligence or educational level. Mid-Southern vowels may be thought of as cute, quaint, or queer, but Mid-Southern syntax to some ears is proof positive of stupidity or retardation. (See what happens when people eat grits, drink moonshine, and marry their cousins?) Syntactic features of Mid-South English are also problematic in the Michigan classroom because they, unlike "accents," appear in written English. When teachers uncritically accept all the falderal about their students' illiteracy—indeed many teachers promulgate these myths—woe be unto the students who "prove" their inability to write a coherent English sentence by producing so-called garbled syntax that is nothing other than perfectly well-formed Mid-South English.[5]

Proportional to the rules constituting our linguistic competence and to the high degree of uniformity required by any language, regional differences in syntax are no doubt linguistically—and communicatively—trivial. Their linguistic insignificance does not mean that they are therefore socially insignificant. Indeed, some would argue that the social significance of a linguistic variant is inversely proportional to its linguistic importance and, further, that social significance is typically a *result* of linguistic insignificance.

Mid-Southern English is characterized by at least ten fairly common syntactic constructions which are not "standard" features of Midwestern English. The catalogue of constructions provided here is not intended to be exclusive or inclusive. Its features have been selected for discussion because they are not socially-marked in the Mid-South but may well be in the Midwest and because each is explainable by a grammatical rule or set of rules affecting types of constructions, not just individual variations. For example, sentence initial *used to*, meaning *formerly* or *in the past*, as in "Used to, we swam in the St. Francis River," is pervasive in Mid-South English, but it would be socially-marked in the Midwest. Such a feature is not included in the list, however, since it is unique; whatever can be said about the syntax of this construction cannot be generalized to cover other combinations of words.

The Double Modal Construction

The first word in a verb phrase can be a modal auxiliary—*can, could, may, might, must, shall, should, will,* and *would.* In mid-South English, however, a verb phrase sometimes has not one but two modals. For instance, in Mid-

South English sentences 1.1 and 1.2 are possible:

1.1 *I might could work.*

1.2 *I might can work.*

Furthermore, the construction *might should*, but never *might shall*, is allowable as in 1.3:

1.3 *I might should have called him.*

Some other double modals are *might can, might would,* and *many can*:

1.4 *It may can be moved.*

Other combinations of modals include the two "semi-modals" *used to* and *ought to* in the grammatical constructions *might ought to, used to could,* and *used to would.* As the first element in a double modal construction, *should* is always negated as in *shouldn't ought to.* Other negative double modals include *might couldn't, might can't, may not can, may not could, might not could, used to couldn't,* and *used to wouldn't.* Both the sequence of tenses and the combination of modals are clearly quite intricate in double modal constructions.

The semantics of modals is not easily explainable. While some double modals differ from single ones, others do not. Thus, sentences 1.5 and 1.6 mean the same thing.

1.5 *I shouldn't ought to go.*

1.6 *I shouldn't go.*

Other double modals, however, are quite different in meaning from single modals. For example, to speakers of Mid-South English for whom double modals are natural, *might could* is unmistakably different from either *might* or *could* used alone. Sentence 1.1 means, "I might be able to work," or "It is possible but not certain that I will be able to work." Similarly, sentence 1.3 means "It is possible but not certain that I ought to have called him."

The Ellipsis of Infinitive Verbs of Motion

Mid-South English differs from other varieties of the language with regard to a number of intricate and restricted rules for sentences with the verb + infinitive phrase construction. One of the most common differences involves the elisions of infinitive verbs-of-motion. The conditions under which these infinitives are deletable are quite specific. The understood subject of the infinitive used as the direct object of the sentence must be identical to the noun phrase which is the subject of the sentence. Such subjects of infinitive phrases are never expressed. The main verb of the sentence must be *want, need,* or a semantically similar verb. The infinitive phrase must consist of a verb of motion (such as *go)* and an adverb of location. Under such conditions sentences of the following type are common in English:

2.1 *I need to go outside.*

2.2 *He wants to get off the horse.*

While both sentences 2.1 and 2.2 occur in Mid-South English, infinitive phrases are also optionally (and usually) subject to a deletion rule that results in these paraphrases:

2.3 I need outside.

2.4 He wants off the horse.

The Ellipsis of to be from Passive Infinitive Phrases

Not so widespread in Mid-South English, but still common with some speakers, is another kind of ellipsis in infinitive constructions. Passive infinitive phrases such as the one in 3.1 can be paraphrased as 3.2.

3.1 *The house needs to be painted.*

3.2 *The house need painted.*

Also grammatical are the following sentences:

3.3 *The baby wants changed.*

3.4 *The dog's dish doesn't need washed.*

3.5 *If your transmission needs rebuilt, they can rebuild it.*

All dialects of English allow for *to be* to be deleted from a passive infinitive phrase when the subject is expressed. Such deletion, for example, allows 3.6 to be paraphrased as 3.7.

3.6 *I want the house to be painted by Joe.*

3.7 *I want the house painted by Joe.*

Mid-South English differs from other dialects in that the deletion of *to be* in passive infinitive phrases is possible even when the subject of the infinitive is not expressed.

The Insertion of for before Subjects of Infinitives Used as Direct Objects

If an infinitive phrase contains a subject and if the phrase is used as a subject of the sentence, it will be introduced with the preposition *for* as in 4.1.

4.1 *For you to live alone takes courage.*

In many dialects if the infinitives with subjects serve other syntactic functions, such as the direct object, these phrases are not introduced with *for*, as in 4.2.

4.2 *I wanted the Philadelphia 76ers to lose to the Lakers.*

In Mid-South English the rules for introducing infinitive phrases with *for* are different. With some verbs such as *like, need, prefer,* and *wish,* the *for* is inserted in Mid-South syntax where other dialects would obligatorily omit it. These sentences are all grammatical in Mid-South English:

4.3 *I like for people to be happy.*
4.4 *I wished for it to rain.*
4.5 *I dislike for children to be spanked.*
4.6 *They prefer for us to stay another week.*

It should be noted that the lexical conditions determining whether the *for* will be used to introduce the infinitive phrase differ widely among speakers of Mid-South English.

The it + *Noun Clause Appositive Construction*

In all dialects of English a sentence like 5.1 may be paraphrased as 5.2.
5.1 *That you were sick was unfortunate.*
5.2 *It was unfortunate that you were sick.*

Linguists disagree about the interpretation of the syntactic structure of sentences like 5.2. One analysis holds that the subject of the sentence is the noun clause *that you were sick*, which has been transposed, and *it* is a mere expletive, a word with no semantic reference, occupying the subject position vacated by the noun clause. Another interpretation holds that the noun clause is in apposition with the pronoun *it* since the clause explains what *it* means. If the appositive analysis is accepted, a peculiarity must be noticed: the appositive noun clause is separated from its related pronoun. In Mid-South English, unlike many other dialects, it is possible for the direct object of a verb to be the pronoun *it* followed by an appositive noun clause or infinitive phrase. Thus, the following are all grammatical in Mid-South syntax:
5.3 *I dislike it for you to smoke marijuana.*
5.4 *I can't guarantee it that we will win.*
5.5 *I hate it that you missed the family reunion.*

Like other dialects, Mid-South English does not allow for the construction of *it* plus a gerund phrase appositive.

The Inversion of Subject and Auxiliary in Indirect Questions

In many English dialects, indirect or embedded questions have structures different from their direct question versions. When *yes/no* questions are embedded, instead of changing the word order, *if* or *whether* is inserted before the question:
6.1 *I want to know if the typewriter will be repaired tomorrow.*
6.2 *I want to know whether the typewriter will be repaired tomorrow.*

In *wh-* questions that are embedded, subject-auxiliary inversion is similarly blocked, but the *wh-* word is still moved to the front of the question structure:

6.3 *I wonder when the typewriter will be repaired.*

6.4 *I don't know how he does that.*

6.5 *She asked where you have been.*

6.6 *Tell me what you found.*

6.7 *Can you tell me where the library is?*

All the preceding statements about indirect questions are true of Mid-South English, but it also has alternative ways of constructing embedded or indirect questions too, as the following sentences illustrate.

6.8 *I want to know will the typewriter be repaired tomorrow.*

6.9 *We are concerned about will it give you the performance you want.*

6.10 *I asked her why didn't she stay until Tuesday.*

6.11 *She asked where have I been.*

6.12 *Linda wanted to know was I OK.*

6.13 *Can you tell me where is the library?*

6.14 *They are going to judge how do we conduct ourselves now.*

6.15 *We ought to investigate what other interests does he have.*

6.16 *You may be wondering where's the best place to buy your shoes.*

Some may conclude that these sentences merely contain quotations of questions which have not been puncuated correctly, but that is not the case. In speech these sentences have intonation patterns markedly different from sentences with direct questions. In addition, the pronouns in the indirect questions often differ in person from those in direct questions and some verb forms are different. For example, if the questions in sentences 6.10 and 6.11 are expressed directly, the resulting sentences take these forms:

6.17 *I asked her, "Why, don't you stay until Tuesday?"*

6.18 *She asked, "Where have you been?"*

The Deletion of Subject Relative Pronouns

If the relative pronouns *who(m), which,* or *that* are not the grammatical subject of the relative clause, they may be deleted:

7.1 *This is a vegetable (which) I dislike.*

7.2 *John has the dog (that) I trained.*

7.3 *Rufus is the person (who[m]) you met.*

It is frequently said that a relative pronoun cannot be deleted if it is the subject of the relative clause, but in Mid-South English, this restriction does not hold. For many speakers of Mid-South English these are all grammatical sentences with relative clauses:

7.4 *He's one of those guys can break boards with his hands.*

7.5 *Harold is the one said you wanted to sell it.*

7.6 *I know a fellow works for the highway department in Little Rock.*

7.7 *She is the kind of woman talks all the time.*
7.8 *There's a lot of people eat possum down there.*
7.9 *He had a boy died on him one year.*
7.10 *They have a quarterback can really throw the football.*
7.11 *There were showers and thunderstorms moved across the region.*

The Use of the Expletive it with a Postponed Subject

English sentences frequently begin with *there is* or *there are* in which *there* does not have a locative interpretation. Examples are 8.1 and 8.2:
8.1 *There is time to eat before we go.*
8.2 *There are several reasons for doing that.*
In both sentences the existential or explicative *there* serves only as a dummy subject for the copula. Of course, many speakers commonly use a contracted *there's* even when the following noun phrase is plural. Mid-South English shares these features with other dialects, but it also contains variant constructions not shared by many other dialects.

Instead of, or in addition to an existential *there*, many speakers of Mid-South English use an existential *it*, as illustrated in the following sentences:
8.3 *It's a pony down at my uncle's farm.*
8.4 *It's a lot to this business.*
8.5 *It's money in raising hogs this year.*
8.6 *It's catfish in that river.*
8.7 *It was a substitute teacher today.*
8.8 *It's still no consensus on the city council about the pay raise.*
In these sentences *it* has no referential meaning, although sentences like 8.3 are ambiguous. In response to a question such as, "What is making that noise?" an appropriate response could be, "It's a pony down at my uncle's farm." In this response, *it* refers to *the pony; It* supplies the answer to *what.* But in Mid-South English 8.3 can be, and usually is, interpreted differently. If this sentence is the first one in a conversation, for example, *it* cannot be interpreted as anything but an expletive.

The Left Dislocation of Noun Phrases

Many teachers and even some textbooks call attention to the so-called double subject construction, reputedly a redundant, ungrammatical construction in which a subject noun phrase is immediately followed by its pronoun, as in 9.1.
9.1 *My brother, he lives in Alabama.*
This is only one type of what is known in linguistics as left dislocation. Appar-

ently in order to focus attention upon a noun phrase in a sentence, speakers of Mid-South English will prepose the noun phrase before the sentence and, following conventional rules for pronominalization, replace the noun phrase in the sentence with the appropriate pronoun. Thus, in addition to double subjects, left dislocation also produces sentences like 9.2 and 9.3.

9.2 *That dog, I never could hunt him.*

9.3 *Clint Eastwood, did you see his last movie?*

The Preposing of Negative Auxiliaries

When a negative sentence has an indefinite pronoun for its subject or when the scope of the negative is confined to the subject of the sentence (as in sentence 10.1), speakers of Mid-Southern English may precede the subject with a contraction of a verbal auxiliary and the word *not* (i.e., *can't, wasn't, didn't, won't*). This construction might be used to convey an emphatic negative:

10.1 *No animal killed that goat.*

As a result, sentences like these are common:

10.2 *Can't anyone fix this lawnmower.*

10.3 *Wasn't nothing wrong with his ankle.*

10.4 *Didn't everybody forget my birthday.*

10.5 *Won't just anybody do that kind of work.*

10.6 *Didn't no animal kill that goat.*

Of course, those constructions with two negative elements enjoy an uncertain status because of the widespread prohibitions against "double negatives," but they are used anyway. Usually, however, there is no similar discomfort in the use of a preposed negative auxiliary when no other negative element is expressed in the sentence.

Native speakers of Mid-South English will use constructions such as the ten discussed in this paper, not only in speech but also in writing. Presumably, if Midwestern teachers hear or observe these constructions in the language of their students, these teachers may experience negative subjective reactions to what are in the minds of the users perfectly "normal" expressions. In spite of a stated tolerance for "accents," these teachers may also feel obliged—with the very best of intentions—to discourage such syntactic constructions in the edited written English of their students. Without knowing precisely how to account for such syntactic "aberrations" or why to reject them, they may proscribe them because they are reputedly wordy, awkward, unclear, unidiomatic, or even ungrammatical.

How adequate are textbooks in helping both Midwestern teachers and students who speak Mid-South English to understand these alleged problems in syntax? Four popular, middle-of-the-road series of texbooks for high school English classes have been examined to determine the adequacy with which they treat these supposedly nonstandard syntactic constructions. The results of this survey are summarized in Table 1. The series are *American English Today*,[6] *Building English Skills*,[7] *English Grammar and Composition*,[8] and *Modern English in Action*.[9] Not one of the books in these series contains an accurate statement of proscription for any of the ten syntactic features under consideration, and only one item—left dislocation—is partially proscribed in three of the series. The *Building English Skills* series contains nothing with respect to left dislocation, but the other three series condemn the resulting "double subject" as a redundancy. None of the books, however, indicates any awareness of other forms of left dislocation. Four syntactic constructions in the list of Mid-South features (indirect questions with subject-auxiliary inversion, infinitive verb-of-motion ellipses, *to be* ellipsis in passive infinitive phrases, and the insertion of *for* before subjects of infinitives used as direct objects) are not treated in any of the books in these series. The five remaining features appear to be sanctioned by the four series of books.

In each of these series of textbooks modals are discussed in treatments of auxiliary verbs, but warnings against double modals are nonexistent. In fact, descriptions of verb phrases vaguely allow for double modal constructions. The following statements are typical of each series:

> "More than one helping verb may come before the main verb." (*AET, The Tools of English*, p. 93)
> "Many verbs . . . consist of a *main verb* and one or more helping verbs or auxiliaries." (*BES, Orange Level*, p. 13)
> "A verb phrase is made up of main verb and one or more *helping verbs*." (*EGC, Complete Course*, p. 13)
> "A verb may be preceded by one, two, or three helping verbs, called 'auxiliaries.' " (*MEA, Book 10, p. 248*)

Clearly, none of these statements proscribes double modal constructions. However, in both the *American English Today* and the *Building English Skills* series, the highest level textbooks describe auxiliary structures in such a way as to limit modals to the first position in verb phrases. The force of such descriptions is seriously diminished since they occur nowhere else in either of the series. Each text in the *American English Today* series contains a chapter entitled "Usage" and each text in the *Building English Skills* series has a chapter on "Verb Usage," but double modals are not discussed in any of these usage chapters.

Neither *American English Today* nor *English Grammar and Composition* contains any information relevant to negative auxiliary preposing, but *Building English Skills* and *Modern English in Action* appear to encourage such con-

Table 1
Treatment of Mid-South Syntax in Selected Textbooks

	AET	BES	EGC	MEA
I. The double modal construction			+	+
II. The ellipsis of infinitive verbs of motion				
III. The ellipsis of *to be* from passive infinitive phrases				
IV. The insertion of *for* before subjects of infinitives used as direct objects				
V. The *it* + noun clause appositive construction				+
VI. The inversion of subject and auxiliary in an indirect question				
VII. The deletion of subject relative pronouns	+	+		+
VIII. The use of the expletive *it* with postponed subjects			+	+
IX. The left dislocation of noun phrases	--		--	--
X. The preposing of negative auxiliaries		+		+

+ = apparent endorsement
– = partial proscription

AET = *American English Today* (McGraw-Hill)
BES = *Building English Skills* (McDougal Little)
EGC = *English Grammar and Composition* (Harcourt Brace Jovanovich)
MEA = *Modern English in Action* (D.C. Heath)

structions. The *Better English Skills* authors tell students that "for emphasis or for a variety of style, the subject is sometimes placed after the verb."[10]According to *Modern English in Action*, "A sentence in which the verb or any part of it comes before the subject is said to be in inverted order."[11] While the author acknowledges that most sentences are constructed in "natural order," teachers are encouraged to teach preposing "for a real understanding of complete subject and complete predicate."[12]In addition, at one point the author advises students that "placing portions of the complete predicate before the subject can provide variety, emphasis, or improvement of sentence rhythm."[13]Certainly, negative auxiliary preposing can achieve all three of these qualities.

Constructions in which the pronoun *it* is followed by an appositive noun clause are not specifically treated in any of the series, but one text in the *Modern English in Action* group discusses a related construction. In a section on the functions of noun clauses, the use of the noun clause as an appositive is illustrated with the following sentence: "By the middle of the twentieth century it became apparent that space travel was feasible." In the subsequent discussion the author explains that the noun clause *that space travel was feasible* is in apposition with the pronoun *it*.[14] Since the author does not specify that the pronoun *it* and the noun clause must be separated for grammatical purposes, the author implies that the following sentence, possible in Mid-South English, is well-formed: "I believed it that space travel was feasible."

In all of these textbook series, the deletion of relative pronouns is described so generally that subject relative pronoun deletion is apparently natural. The following accounts of relative pronoun deletion are typical:

> "In many relative clauses (especially in *spoken* English, the relative pronoun has been *omitted*. This typically happens when the pronoun would have stood for the object of the clause." (*AET, The Uses of English*, p. 153)
> "A majority of the adjective clauses in modern writing begin with an introductory word. There is a growing tendency, however, to use adjective clauses with no introductory word." (*BES, Purple Level*, pp. 88-89)
> "In some cases the relative pronoun is omitted." (*EGC, Fourth Course*, p. 85)
> "Sometimes the relative pronoun is omitted." (*MEA, Book 9*, p. 430)

Despite hedges such as "sometimes," "in some cases," "a majority," and "typically," none of the texts state that subject relative pronoun deletion is ungrammatical, nonstandard, casual, or confusing; by implication it is as natural as the deletion of any other relative pronoun.

The use of *it* as an expletive is not covered in *American English Today* or *Building English Skills*, but the other series seem to approve it as a substitute for *there*. In *English Grammar and Composition*, the expletive function of *it* and *there* is discussed in a single paragraph. The illustrative sentence, *"There are arguments on both sides,"* is followed with this explanation:

"In this use *there* is called an expletive, a word used to get the sentence stated. The word *it* may also be used as an expletive: 'it was useless to argue.' " (*EGC, Complete Course*, p. 26)

Whether *it* and *there* are interchangeable is unclear, but the possibility is certainly suggested. According to *Modern English in Action*, however, there is no question about whether *it* may be used for *there* in the expletive construction, for the author writes:

"In sentences such as 'It snowed every day last week' and 'Wasn't it an exciting game!' *it* is used without antecedent." (*MEA, Book 10*, p. 375)

If in the sentence, "Wasn't it an exciting game!" *it* is interpreted as an expletive and not a subject pronoun with *an exciting game* as its subjective complement, then the sentence could be paraphrased as "Wasn't there an exciting game!" Thus, *it* and *there*, according to this text, are interchangeable expletives.

If these four series of high school textbooks are typical (and I have no reason to believe that they are not), students in Midwestern classrooms for whom Mid-South syntax is natural face the hazard of being victimized by texbook writers and teachers. If a Midwestern teacher red pencils any features of Mid-South syntax discussed in this paper, those "offending" students may perceive that for no legitimate reason their natural language is being singled out for censure. They may suspect that their teachers are simply prejudiced against them. Even if those students passively and uncritically accept the Midwestern teacher's accusation that their natural Mid-Southern syntax is "nonstandard," turning to the textbook will provide almost no explanation of the "nonstandardness" of their syntax nor guidance for "correctness." Given students' tendency to accept textbooks as larger authorities than their teachers, students may be puzzled by what they discover in those textbooks. Instead of proscribing the syntactic constructions rejected by Midwestern teachers, the books in many instances appear to endorse supposedly unacceptable English. Given this situation, if those students whose Mid-Southern English has been rejected suspect their Midwestern teachers of prejudice, the texts provide evidence to confirm those suspicions. It seems only reasonable to conclude that likely responses to such discoveries would be additional hostility toward Midwestern teachers and further alienation from the education system. To assure these students of their rightful educational opportunities to "build on and take advantage of the cultural and linguistic heritage,"[15] students whose English has Mid-South features will require, at the very least, better curriculum materials than are presently available and teachers who are linguistically and culturally sophisticated with respect to those students whose heritage is rooted in the Mid-South.

NOTES

1. For example, even though I am a sociolinguist and know better, when I hear someone from the Detroit area talk, I register a variety of negative, occasionally hostile reactions, and I know why. When I was growing up in a small town in northeast Arkansas the only people I knew from the Detroit area were the children and grandchildren of local folks who had gone North to work in the automobile plants. When those kids would visit relatives in Arkansas, they came down in Buicks and Cadillacs; they wore better clothes and had more money than we did. They ridiculed everyone and everything from Arkansas, and we Arkansawyers despised them mightily. Given a previously inculcated dislike for damn Yankees, was it any wonder that we developed negative attitudes toward people who talked like they were from Detroit?

2. Halloran, J.D. *Attitude formation and change, television research committee working paper no. 2.* Leicester: Leicester University Press, 1967, pp.60-61, 68. See also Galvan, Jose L., Pierce, James A., Underwood, Gary N. The relevance of selected educational variables of teachers to their attitudes toward Mexican American English. *Journal of the Linguistic Association of the Southwest*, 1976, *2* (1), 13-27.

3. Galvan, Jose L., Pierce, James A. and Underwood, Gary N. Relationships between teacher attitudes and differences in the English of bilinguals. In *Swallow IV: Linguistics and Education, Proceedings of the Fourth Annual Southwest Area Language and Linguistics Workshop.* San Diego: Institute for Cultural Pluralism, 1976, pp. 279-314. See also Williams, Frederick and Whitehead, Jack L., Language in the classroom: Studies in the Pygmalion effect. *The English Record*, 1971, *21* (4), 108-113 and Frederick Williams et al., *Explorations of the linguistic attitudes of teachers.* Rowley, Massachusetts: Newbury House, 1976.

4. The Detroit school experience of Bob Thomas, now a professor of Anthropology at Wayne State University, is poignantly retold in McDavid, Raven I., Sense and nonsense about American dialect users. In Harold B. Allen & Gary N. Underwood (Eds.), *Readings in American dialectology*. New York: Appleton-Century-Crofts, 1971, pp. 39-40. See also Golden, Ruth I., *Improving patterns of language usage.* Detroit: Wayne State University Press, 1960.

5. Do you think I'm kidding? When I was in graduate school at the University of Minnesota, prose which had served me with distinction through eighteen years of education in Arkansas and Texas was suddenly pounced upon by otherwise reasonable and intelligent professors as being occasionally downright un-English. When I realized that they were merely reacting to my Mid-Southern English, I defiantly began loading the essays I wrote for those professors with every cornpone construction I could think of. Somehow, I managed to earn my degree anyway.

6. Hans P. Guth (ed.), *American English today,* 2nd ed., New York: Webster Divi-

sion/McGraw-Hill, 1975. Volumes examined for the present study are subtitled *The Tools of English, The Uses of Language,* and *Our Changing Language.*

7.   The Staff of the Writing Improvement Project. *Building English Skills.* Evanston: McDougal, Littell & Co., 1977. Volumes examined for the present study are identified as the Orange, Blue Yellow, and Purple levels.

8.   Warriner, John E., Whitten, Mary E., Griffith, Francis. *English and composition.* Heritage edition. New York: Harcourt Brace Jovanovich, 1977. Volumes studied for the present study are identified as the Third, Fourth, Fifth, and Complete courses.

9.   Christ, Henry I. *Modern English in action.* Boston: D.C. Heath, 1965. Volumes examined for the present study are identified as books 9 through 12.

10.   *Orange Level,* pp. 54 and 56; *Blue Level,* p. 52; and *Yellow Level,* p. 55.

11.   Book 9, p. 272; Book 10, p. 250; Book 11, p. 261; and Book 12, p. 252.

12.   Book 9, teachers' edition, p. 272.

13.   Book 10, p. 251.

14.   Book 12, p. 290. The construction is illustrated with similar sentences in other books in this series.

15.   Letter received from John Chambers, Reading and Language Studies Program for Teaching and Learning, National Institute of Education, dated May 9, 1980.

REFERENCES

Chambers, John. Letter to the author. 9 May 1980.

Christ, Harry I. *Modern English in action.* Boston: D.C. Heath, 1965.

Galvan, Jose L., Pierce, James A., and Underwood, Gary N. Relationships between teacher attitudes and differences in the English of bilinguals. In *SWALLOW IV: Linguistics and Education. Proceedings of the Fourth Annual Area Language and Linguistics Workshop.* San Diego: Institue for Cultural Pluralism, 1976.

Galvan, Jose L., Pierce, James A. and Underwood, Gary N. The relevance of selected educational variables of teachers to their attitudes toward Mexican American English. *Journal of the Linguistic Association of the Southwest,* 1976, *2* (1), 13-27.

Golden, Ruth I. *Improving patterns of language usage.* Detroit: Wayne State University Press, 1960.

Guth, Hans (Ed.), *American English today.* 2nd ed. New York: Webster Division/McGraw-Hill, 1973.

Halloran, J.D. *Attitude formation and change.Television research committee working paper no. 2.* Leicester: Leicester University Press, 1967.

McDavid, Raven I., Jr. Sense and nonsense about American dialects. In Harold B. Allen & Gary N. Underwood (Eds.), *Readings in American dialectology.* New York: Appleton-

Century-Crofts, 1971.

The Writing Improvement Project. *Building English skills.* Evanston: McDougal, Littell & Co., 1977.

Warriner, John E., Whitten, Mary E., & Griffith, Francis. *English grammar and composition.* Heritage Edition. New York: Harcourt Brace Jovanovich, 1977.

Williams, Frederick & Whitehead, Jack L., Language in the classroom: Studies in the Pygmalion effect. *The English Record*, 1971, *21* (4), 108-113.

Williams, Frederick et al. *Explorations of the linguistic attitudes of teachers.* Rowley, Massachusetts: Newbury House, 1976.

THE BLACK ENGLISH CONTROVERSY AND ITS IMPLICATIONS FOR ADDRESSING THE EDUCATIONAL NEEDS OF BLACK CHILDREN: THE CULTURAL LINGUISTIC APPROACH

Judith A. Starks

Ms. Starks is the Program Director for the Cultural Linguistic Approach and an instructor in the Department of Inner City Studies at Northeastern Illinois University, Chicago, Illinois. She has been instrumental in the development of the Cultural Linguistic instructional mode, and responsible for its introduction in numerous school systems throughout the United States.

ₓThe effect the Black child's language has on his or her potential for academic achievement has been the particular focus of educational, linguistic and sociological research and discussion for the past two decades. The legitimacy of Black English continues to be hotly debated and it appears that the emotions underlying the arguments on all sides remain very deep.

‗ Judge Charles Joiner, presiding over the controversial Ann Arbor "Black English" case, ruled that teachers must take into account the features of Black English and Black childrens' culture when planning their instruction. Not to do so, he argued, would perpetuate educational barriers to Black children's academic achievement. As school systems in Ann Arbor and elsewhere seek programs complying with Judge Joiner's decision, there are a few programs already in existence which effectively address the needs of Black children. One such program is the Cultural Linguistics Approach, which has operated in public school systems since 1969.

This paper invites a closer look at the theory and methodology of the Cultural Linguistic Approach. The program can be best understood in relationship to the controversy surrounding the *King* decision, the *deficit/difference* schools of thought which shaped instruction of Black children in the sixties and seventies, and the development of a rationale for cultural pluralism and effective multiethnic educational programs. The first three sections of this paper will therefore provide these historical perspectives for the last section, which offers an overview of the Cultural Linguistic Approach.

Black English: The King *Case and its Repercussions*

He can't yet read and probably just learned to write his name. His basic desires are neither fancy nor unrealistic. He likes candy bars and ice cream and probably plays games with his broccoli. He has trouble lacing up his shoes, buttoning small buttons, and he can't be left alone in the house. He's only five years old, yet he's the most talked about, conjectured about, researched about and lied about entity in American educational, social and political arenas today. Reputations and fortunes have been made and lost because of him. He is the Black child, and he is being mis-educated, under-educated or not educated by all of the best intentions in the world! (1980, p. 30)

The Black child, so eloquently described above by Naomi Millender, has recently been the focus of a controversy centering on the landmark decision made in the case of the *Martin Luther King Junior Elementary School Children, et al., vs. Ann Arbor School District Board.* The case was brought by parents of eleven Black students ranging in age from 6 to 13 and living in Ann Arbor's Green Road Housing Project. These parents accused school officials at Martin Luther King, Jr. Elementary School of insensitivity to the indigenous speech of Black students. These students had been classified as needing speech therapy or as learning-disabled by the school. Parents demanded that school authorities "recognize" Black English as a formal and distinct dialect with an historical and cultural basis and its own grammatical structure. The plaintiffs argued that, in the process of determining students' eligibility for special education services, the Ann Arbor School District Board has failed to ascertain whether learning difficulties stemmed from cultural, social and economic deprivations—deprivations which, the plaintiffs alleged, prevented them from making normal progress in school.

In July 1979, after three weeks of argument, U.S. District Judge Charles W. Joiner ruled that the district must recognize Black English, the language most Black students speak at home. Joiner also ordered the district to develop a program helping teachers to recognize this language and take it into account in teaching standard English to speakers whose indigenous language is Black English. In so doing, he observed that there was a failure on the part of the school board to provide leadership and help for its teachers in learning about the existence of Black English as a home and community language of many Black students. He also recognized that the board had failed to offer teachers methods of using that knowledge in teaching Black children code-switching skills for reading standard English, and that inattention to the relationship between Black English and standard English was not rational in light of existing knowledge on the subject (Monteith, 1980). The district was given thirty days to submit a plan indicating how it would comply with the court order.

During the trial, experts in linguistics and education gave testimony on some of the characteristic features of Black English. Though the key testimony convinced Judge Joiner that indeed a *language barrier* existed which impeded equal participation by its students in its instructional programs, he threw out five of the six claims of violations which the plaintiffs sought to establish. The rejected claims held that cultural, social and economic deprivations prevented students, in varying degrees, from making normal progress in school. The one claim substantiated through the language barrier argument was that the students' right to equal educational opportunity had been violated by the school board.

In his decision Joiner stated, "If a barrier exists because of the language used by the children in this case, it exists not because the teachers and students cannot understand each other, but because in the process of attempting to teach students how to speak standard English the students are made somehow to feel inferior and are thereby turned off from the learning process" (1979, p. 26). I will elaborate on Joiner's observation later in this paper, because it is one of the constructs which forms the philosophic foundation for the Cultural Linguistic Approach.

Deceptively simple, this must be among the most misunderstood rulings of the decade. Interpretations have ranged from expecting Black English to be taught in school, to forcing the use of a dual language system, to teaching teachers to speak Black English. Of course the misunderstandings are only symptomatic of the complexity of societal factors germane to, but not directly affected by the judge's decision.

Joiner's decision certainly has stimulated a rash of responses—some thoughtful, others hysterical. An article in *Crisis* magazine evokes the emotional intensity with which the implications of the decision is debated:

> The new cult of blackness has spawned many astounding vagaries, most of them harmless, some of them intriguing and others merely amusing. One which has recently gained a measure of academic and foundation recognition is not only sheer nonsense[Ebonics] but also a cruel hoax which,if allowed to go unchallenged, can cripple generations of Black youngsters in their preparation to compete in the open market with their non-Negro peers (Seymour & Seymour, 1979, p. 401).

Donald F. McHenry, former U.S. Ambassador to the United Nations and a public speaking instructor at Howard University, offers his opinion on the Black English controversy:

> "I do not approve of Black English. In the first place, I do not understand it; in the second place, I think the objective of education is to lead out. I think that in our society—though we ought to take advantage of the cultural differences that really make Americans American—we ought to

eliminate those differences which are either the basis or result of divisiveness in our society" (McHenry, 1980, p. 40).

Another negative reaction to the court's ruling comes from journalist Carl Rowan. He refers to Black English as "silly," and deplores what he views as the court's efforts to declare Black English a foreign language, to be used to help Blacks learn algebra, physics, and biology:

> What black children need is an end to this malarkey that tells them they can fail to learn grammar, fail to develop vocabularies, ignore syntax and embrace the mumbo-jumbo of ignorance—and dismiss it in the name of "black pride."

> What we need is massive allocation of teachers and resources to remedial programs to teach black children to speak, read and write the language of their native land. (Rowan, 1979, p. 36).

On the other side of the issue, James Baldwin believes that the argument has nothing to do with language itself, but with the role of language. He believes that people use language in order to describe and control their circumstances. For Baldwin, language is a political instrument crucial to one's identity. He sees the problem as rooted in American history:

> A people at the center of the Western world, and in the midst of so hostile a population, has not endured and transcended by means of what is patronizingly called a "dialect." We, the blacks, are in trouble, certainly, but we are not doomed, and we are not inarticulate because we are not compelled to defend a morality that we know to be a lie. The brutal truth is that the bulk of the white people in America never had any interest in educating black people, except as this could serve white purposes. It is not the black child's language that is in question, it is not his language that is despised: It is his experience. A child cannot be taught by anyone who despises him, and a child cannot afford to be fooled. A child cannot be taught by anyone whose demand, essentially is that the child repudiate his experience, and all that gives him sustenance, and enter a limbo in which he will no longer be black, and in which he knows that he can never become white. Black people have lost too many black children that way (Baldwin, 1979, p. E19).

Syndicated columnist William Rasberry, though essentially in agreement with Rowan, did have some different observations after reading Baldwin's article. He commented that the issue is no longer one of definitions, but of what the schools plan to do about Black English. He observed that the answer to the problem would vary with the skills, attitudes and personalities of individual teachers and he proposed two essential considerations:

> First, teachers must learn and keep reminding themselves, that the child who comes to school speaking Black English (or any other dialect) is not on that account less intelligent, less admirable or less anything else than

the child whose home language is standard English.

Second, they must understand and convey to their children, that while it is necessary to learn standard English for use in the classroom or on the job, other dialects may be more appropriate for other circumstances (Rasberry, 1979, sec. 3, p. 3).

Dr. Orlando Taylor, a Howard University linguist, is amazed that, in comparison to the Black English controversy, which has been discussed and argued by scholars and educational practitioners for so long, other social dialects have rarely been considered. Where are the discussions about such dialects as Polish English, German English, Jewish English, Appalachian English, and so on? He notes:

> In all societies with writing systems, there are prestigious language varieties which obtain currency as the language of education. These prestige varieties may be referred to as the standard variety of that language. A situation of this type exists in the United States, resulting in the concept of standard English. We must destroy the myth that it is a single variety of rather pedantic English, spoken by English teachers and Walter Cronkite. Further, standard English is not white English. There are many varieties of prestige or standard English spoken in the United States, including varieties spoken by black Americans (Taylor, 1980, p.22).

Continuing, Taylor offers a key observation on which the misinterpretation of Joiner's order hinges:

> To not *teach* a particular community dialect is not the same as to deny that dialect from being used in the schools as a vehicle to teach the child the language of education. Nor does it mean the child shouldn't be permitted opportunities to become even more proficient in using the dialect in those situations where it is appropriate. Schools have the responsibility to teach the language of education to every student. However, this teaching should not be done in such a way as to deny the importance of native community dialects (p. 22).

Other linguists share Taylor's view that clinging to the notion of standard English is part of the problem. Robbins Burling observes that when we are contemptuous of people, we tend to be contemptuous of their language. Following Taylor, Burling states that no one feels uncomfortable, for example, at the suggestion that a special dialect of English is peculiar to Ireland and that we can talk about the Irish dialect without implying inferiority:

> It is a tribute to our educational system that the overwhelming majority of Americans have been instilled with a rock-like conviction that certain linguistic forms are correct, while others are wrong . . . This "conventional" wisdom is wrong. As we have seen, there are usually many ways of saying the same thing, and there is no possible way of determining in every case that just one of the alternatives is correct. Variability is a permanent

fact of language (Burling, 1973, p. 130).

Some experts have been even more candid in their assessment of the insistence on standard English and have argued that the issue is loaded with racism and elitism. Betty Lou DuBois asserts:

> Thus it ought to be clear that the imposition of a standard is as much of a class as a racial matter, racism becoming a factor only after the school years. As others pointed out, implicit in the imposition of a standard dialect is the premise that it is language that bars upward mobility within the social structure: if only you learn to speak like us, we will accept you. Ceteris paribus, many have found this to be true. Others, among them Blacks and Chicanos, have found it largely a cruel hoax: the effort and suffering attendant on rejection of self and group identity have not been rewarded by free passage into the mainstream. There is probably very little the schools can do to change the prevalent attitudes of the dominant group, since the schools are after all its agents, but they can cease promoting the belief that mastery of standard dialect insures entry into the dominant group (1977, p. 294).

Nuru (1980) observes that societal attitudes attached to Black dialect (and many other varieties of English) transcend the linguistic competence of that dialect, permeate the entire world of the child and affect the realization of the child's aspirations. She notes that these attitudes cannot be lightly dismissed or easily changed, and that the reality for the child is that these attitudes later may serve as a basis for academic placement, education and employment.

Naomi Millender's (1980) research in the field of language has led her to conclude that Black language has been equated with the speech of ignorance:

> There has been a conspiracy to ridicule Black language (hence, Black culture) so that even the people who speak it grow ashamed of it. No other language has been so disgraced. We must ask ourselves why English spoken with a French accent (like the French chef) or spoken with a German accent (like ex-secretary of state Henry Kissinger) is tolerated, even admired, while English spoken with a Black accent is despised. And "Black accent" transcends even Black people. As William Stewart observed several years ago, the "southern accent" spoken by whites is as much affected by the African language system as Black speakers in the south have been affected by "middle English." This author doesn't wonder why a southern president like Lyndon B. Johnson or James E. Carter is ridiculed by the media. The same media that artificially offers "Walter Cronkite" speech (a *written* language) as the American standard language could never tolerate an English dialect that even remotely sound like a Negro dialect (p. 35).

Expanding on her findings on the belief that Black English equals ignorance she states,

> This belief is held even today, by those Blacks in positions of knowledge, most peculiarly by many Blacks in the arts and the communication fields. Dr. Geneva Smitherman, a noted Afro-American linguist, included a 1933

quote by Dr. Carter G. Woodson on the subject of Black talk in her recent book:

> "In the study of language in school pupils were made to scoff at the Negro dialect as some peculiar possession of the Negro which they should despise rather than directed to study the background of this language as broken down (i.e., linguistically polluted by English/African tongue)—in short to understand their own linguistic history, which is certainly more important for them than the study of French phonetics or Historical Spanish Grammar."

I have purposely used the term "most peculiarly" when referring to Blacks in the artistic and communicative fields, because they should be the most progressive in any discussion about language or communication styles. What we have observed, however, is often the opposite course. In 1979, particularly in light of the (Ann Arbor) Michigan court case regarding Black language, the most vocally opposed to the legitimacy of Black speech have been our communication specialists—namely our journalists and broadcasters! Instead of advocating the serious in-group study suggested by Dr. Woodson in the above quote, many in this group of journalists have merely added to the confusion; their outcries and lambasts about Black speech have further added credence to the position of the Black linguistic/cultural deficiencies. And, not to let our creative artists off the hook, when will our writers, poets, playwrights, and other authors make some definitive statements in support of the richness of Black language? Do they know the great debt all of America's artists owe to Black culture as captured through its language (p.32-33)?

Millender's observations are right on target. Even one year after the Ann Arbor decision, the Black community still remains divided on the issue of the legitimacy of Black English. It seems that for Blacks it is an issue about which one does not vacillate. It is an issue tied deeply to the hearts and souls of Black folks, inextricably twined into the network of cultural experiences. It is more understandable that a journalist like Carl Rowan would refer to Black English as the "mumbo-jumbo of ignorance" if we recognize the generation and experiential background from which he comes. Most upwardly mobile Blacks of his generation clung steadfastly to the notion that speaking "the King's English" would open the door to opportunity. Rowan's own column lambasting Black English exhibits the schizophrenia experienced by many Blacks who feel they have integrated into American society. On one hand, he demands equal rights for Blacks, yet on the other he deplores a very fundamental characteristic of Black people.

Donald McHenry's comments are also curious. He claims not to understand Black English, yet he is a former public speaking instructor, trained in the fields of language and communication. Surely the effects of racism and oppression are apparent if one who has access to the body of reseach on the origins and features of Black English cannot accept the legitimacy of the language form spoken by the majority of Blacks in this country. To not understand Black English is to not understand Black people!

We cannot fault Rowan for emphasizing the importance of communication and the need for Blacks to have access to the media and marketplace. What he and so many others like him fail to understand is that, as DuBois has pointed out, the promise of the rights and privileges attendant upon full citizenship for Blacks (and I venture to say other non-white ethnics) is a *cruel hoax*. As James Baldwin so clearly explained, Black language itself is not the problem; *It is the Black experience which is despised.* William Rasberry echoes Baldwin's views:

> While it is true that many teachers equate nonstandard English with low intelligence, language is just one of the cues from which conclusions are drawn.
>
> The negative judgements about children from the culture of the slums are made almost as much on how they look and behave as on their speech patterns. Requiring teachers to recognize nonstandard English as a consistent, valid, noninferior language will prevent neither those negative judgements nor their academic consequences. What Kaimowitz [the plaintiffs' attorney] is really demanding is that teachers be sensitive and intelligent, that they avoid negative stereotyping, and that they teach children without infusing them with the feeling of inferiority.

It will take more than a lawsuit to accomplish that (1979, sec. 3, p. 3)

Before moving on to review the larger body of research and theory of which the Black English controversy is a focal point, we can conclude this discussion by considering how the attitudinal problem described by Rasberry can be attacked. If we look at a synopsis of the "plan" offered by the Ann Arbor School district for compliance with Joiner's ruling, we see a short-term solution for a long-term problem. The district provided an in-service program for professional staff at the King Elementary School. Teachers were to receive a minimum of twenty hours of instruction in general language and dialect concepts, including a contrastive analysis of features of Black English speakers, and the use of knowledge of dialect differences to help individual students learn to read standard English. This is quite an agenda, one which has taken linguists many years to master! Staff were also to receive follow-up seminars and a full-time language arts consultant.

As Nuru observes:

> A 20-hour crash course to the tune of $42,000 on "sensitivity" and acceptance of the "linguistic problem" of Black dialect will undoubtedly produce some *instant authorities* on Black English, but *it will not change the complexity of ignorant and perverse attitudes held about race and so-*

*cial class that served in the first place as the basis for destructive colonial-
ist action in establishing white dialect as the standard language by which
all else is to be compared and subordinated.* Any other language would
have done just as well (1980, p. 17).

Nuru and other scholars currently feel that, having established the legitimacy
of the language through expert research, the Black English controversy should
focus on what to do about Black English. Yet the reactions of Carl Rowan
and Donald McHenry, let alone the untapped attitudes of the average white
citizen, are evidence that there is not yet uniformity of thought on the issue.

Black Children: Cultural Deficit or Cultural Difference?

Irreparable harm has come to this [the Black] child because experts have
labeled him cognitively deficient; "experts" have labeled his mother a
lazy baby-maker and his father (when they concede that he has one) as a
deserter. His rich experiences are called non-experiences; his vast history
and complex culture are non-culture or sub-culture; his language is non-
language; and subsequently, he is a non-person. Anyone who is an educat-
or, a parent or a student knows the extensive vocabulary which surrounds
this child, follows him to school, sits in the seat with him and, ultimately,
speaks for him even when he thinks he is speaking for himself. Some of
the words are culturally disadvantaged, the urban disadvantaged, socially
disadvantaged, culturally deprived, experience poor, educationally under-
privileged, the disaffected, children with limited backgrounds, and sometimes just plain "sick" (Millender, 1980, p. 30).

The study of Black American speech has attained unprecedented promi-
nence in the last decade. Educators, linguists and social scientists have focused their research on the Black child's language, with particular emphasis on
nonstandard dialect and its relationship to reading. Studies have looked at a
number of variables in this process—including the child, the instructional materials, and the teacher. Following is an analysis of the two schools of thought
prevalent in the late sixties and throughout the seventies regarding the Black
child and his language.

According to Granger (1976), the early childhood educational establishment's concern for teaching all children to speak standard English has been
based upon a series of myths and assumptions which do not have empirical or
ethical support. In his work with large numbers of early childhood education
practitioners, he has noted that untested assumptions are still current:

(1) Speakers of nonstandard dialects will fail in school since teachers will
not be able to understand; (2) The parents of nonstandard English speaking Black children want their children to speak standard English early in
life;(3) Persons who do not speak standard English will not succeed in the
society at large; and (4) Once it is decided that a young child should learn

to speak standard English, the task of teaching it is a possible one for the preschool or primary teacher (p. 481).

He argues that the need to examine these assumptions is paramount, since many early childhood curriculum developers and practitioners continue their efforts to make nonstandard speaking children speak standard English based upon one or more of the above statements. These developers act as if the statements were empirical truths. According to Granger, all of the assumptions, however, are either unsupported conventional wisdom or contradictory to existing evidence.

Granger investigated the theory popular during the late sixties that nonstandard dialects represent inferior versions of standard English. Such prominent "deficit" theorists as Roger Hess, Virginia Shipman, Martin Deutsch, Carl Bereiter, and Siegfried Englemann predicated their research on the assumption that nonstandard speakers possessed inadequate intelligence and were not capable of abstract forms of reasoning because dialectal forms of language are the result of a restricted code. Based on this logic, some educators believed that nonstandard dialects had to be eradicated from a student's language repetoire before he could learn to read. This type of reasoning has historical precedents in the prescriptive dicta of eighteenth century grammarians who believed that language was correct or incorrect, good or bad (Pietras, 1979).

This language "deficit" viewpoint evolved from the work of Basil Bernstein (1961) who, in the early sixties, suggested the existence of restricted and elaborated language codes in lower and middle socioeconomic classes, respectively, in England. Bernstein viewed the children from the lower socio-economic group as speakers of a restricted code which did not allow them to communicate complex relationships, make hypotheses about the future, or rationales for the present. He viewed the children's code as largely descriptive rather than analytical and stated that the deficient code decreased the speaker's chances for academic success.

Although Bernstein later changed his views on restricted and elaborated codes, American researchers further developed the concept of language deficit and began applying it to speakers of nonstandard English rather than to socioeconomic groups (Dillingofski, 1979). Martin Deutsch (1963) postulated inadequacies in vocabulary and syntax in Black children's speech. M.H. Black (1965) claimed that Black children do not even understand the concept that objects have names. Arthur Jensen (1969) argued that most Blacks do not have cognitive ability to work with abstract concepts, including language processing. Englemann (1970) asserted that Black children have no knowledge of basic linguistic concepts and are unfamiliar with commonplace words. His work, along with that of his colleague Carl Bereiter, led to the creation of a language and reading program for preschool and primary school children for use prior to and in conjunction with initial reading instruction (Kachuck, 1978).

As the literature on deficiency theory flourished, other schools approached the problem of the Black child's language from another perspective. Sociolinguists suggested that the Black child's language is not *deficient*, but merely *different* from standard English. The work of William Labov, Roger Shuy, Joan Baratz, Ralph Fasold and Walt Wolfram focused on the linguistic differences between standard and nonstandard varieties of English. The linguists' research showed systematic dialect patterns in oral language of Black children, thus demonstrating that Black English is a complete language communication system, not an inferior dialect. A precise description of these differences was considered a prerequisite to the development of adequate language programs for Black children. Wolfram found that in 1964 the Center for Applied Linguistics set a precedent by approaching Black English as sufficiently different from standard English to warrant instructional materials for Blacks which utilized foreign language methods. Further, the work of Stewart and Baratz concluded that there is sufficient difference between some nonstandard varieties and standard English to warrant the use of readers written in the Black vernacular (Wolfram, 1974).

As the body of work on linguistic differences between Black English and standard English grew, linguists, educators, and society at large began to focus on the validity of cultural differences. The climate of the sixties and the early seventies gave rise to the acceptance of the notion of cultural diversity, thus upsetting Gunnar Myrdal's theory that America is a giant "melting pot" where ethnic differences are lost as immigrants seek to become American. Suddenly it was acceptable to display pride in one's heritage and to emphasize differences among racial and ethnic groups. With the concept of cultural pluralism came the advocacy of multi-ethnic or multi-cultural instructional materials to highlight each ethnic group's unique characteristics and contributions to American society.

For Blacks, the difference thesis meant that the behaviors of Black Americans were rooted in history and cultural tradition, instead of nurtured by a segregated and hostile society. Though the concept of difference was acceptable for white ethnics, according to the Seymours, applying this notion to Blacks was perceived by the general public as a threat which, if unopposed, could seriously handicap progress toward racial parity:

> To espouse cultural difference rather than deficiency challenged prevailing notions of the Black man's problem, a position untenable to Black and white people who wished to change qualities they regarded as disadvantaging to Black people. Despite objections to the concept of linguistic difference, it was an idea whose time had come. While many Black Americans

were opposed to the concept, there were many more who found it particularly compatible with the other newly acquired notions such as Black is
Beautiful and Powerful; concepts that would have been viewed as ludi-
crous just a few years earlier. (Seymour & Seymour, 1979, p. 401).

The cultural difference theory affected the teaching of English as dialects
were identified by particular sets of grammatical and phonological features. In
1974, the Executive Committee of the Conference on College Composition
And Communication (CCCC) adopted a resolution generally accepted in the
English profession, which recognized the student's right to his or her own language:

> We affirm the students' right to their own patterns and varieties of lan-
> guage—the dialects of their nurture or whatever dialects in which they find
> their own identity and style. Language scholars long ago denied that the
> myth of a standard American dialect has any validity. The claim that any
> one dialect is unacceptable amounts to an attempt of one social group to
> exert its dominance over another. Such a claim leads to false advice for
> humans. A nation proud of its diverse heritage and its cultural and racial
> variety will preserve its heritage of dialects. We affirm strongly that teach-
> ers must have the experiences and training that will enable them to respect
> diversity and uphold the right of students to their own language (Corbett,
> 1974, p. 203).

Karen Schuster-Webb (1980) notes that despite evidence to the contrary,
the schools and society still interpret Black English as a barrier to learning
because it is viewed as a product of a disadvantaged or nonexistent culture.
She sees the reaction to the CCCC statement as fostering an eradicationist
viewpoint advocating the elimination of Black English in favor of what is referred to as standard American English. She notes that moderate intervening
viewpoints still de-emphasize the use of dialect in the educational setting:

> Many educators, however, are unfamiliar with linguists' analyses of Black
> English or other American English dialects and simply dismiss these
> speech forms as undesirable. The fault does not lie completely with the
> educators, however; conflicting nomenclature, debates among creolist and
> dialect proponents, and the research void in the areas of voice register, in-
> tonation, and lexical repertoire have all added to the confusion surround-
> ing Black English (p.90)

Curiously enough, out of the *deficit/difference* controversy has come
largely the same remedy. The *deficit* theorists recommended an eradication of
the dialect they viewed as inferior (Black English) as soon as the Black child
reached nursery school age. The *difference* theorists, while not placing quite
so strong an emphasis on rejecting Black English, still advocated the use of instructional materials designed to achieve the same end as the *deficit* theory advocates—i.e, to teach the child to speak standard English. The fact remains
that by exposure either to Engelmann's structured pattern drills (*deficit*) or to

the dialect readers and Teaching English as a Second Language techniques of Steward, Baratz, Shuy, et al. (*difference*), the Black child is still expected to change *his* identity (of which his language is an essential component) to conform to the school and its method of instruction. While we consider the pragmatic value of learning standard English in this society, we must again recall Betty Lou DuBois' caution and the words of James Baldwin. Clothed in the mantle of *deficit* or *difference*, our scholars are still prescribing a remedy which smacks of racism and elitist notions. Where, then, is the answer to the question of providing equal educational opportunity to Black children without requiring them to strip themselves of their very identity? Again we must refer to the Cultural Linguistic Approach which will be described in detail later in this paper. In laying the groundwork for understanding such a program, it is important to go deeper into the Black English controversy and review some of the research on the relationship between Black English and reading ability.

Black English and Reading

Deficit and *difference* theorists alike have postulated that the Black child's language and the language of print are different and that the mismatch between the two causes interference when the Black child learns to read. The interference points have been identified as phonological, syntactic and semantic. This resulting mismatch is offered as the cause for the high rate of reading failure among children who speak nonstandard English.

A variety of research in the mid-seventies concentrated on the interference between Black English and learning to read standard English material. Early research on dialect interference led to widespread advocacy among *difference* theorists of using dialect as a "bridge" to teach standard English. A commercial reading series by that name was developed in 1977 by Gary Simpkins, Grace Holt and Charlesetta Simpkins. The authors believe that simplifying the task of reading for underachieving Black English speakers (at the level of junior and senior high school) is accomplished through first introducing written materials in Black vernacular, and then gradually introducing standard English. Stories are written in Black English, with standard English counterparts. From Black English to standard English, students read parallel stories in Black English, transitional form and standard English. Criticisms of this series have centered on the unexpected emphasis on oral reading in the upper grades, and on whether or not a non-Black English speaking teacher can do a credible job with the material (Lass, 1978).

The work of Sims (1975) also establishes some problems with the dialect interference theory. Sims debunks the notion that teachers do not understand their Black English speaking students, and that Black English speaking students do not or cannot understand their teachers:

> First, more attention should be devoted to the differences between receptive and productive language processes, and the competence needed to use them effectively. Since reading is a receptive process, a reader does not need to be able to speak a dialect in order to read it. That is, a speaker of Black dialect can learn to read standard written English without becoming a speaker of standard English. It seems likely, however, that, in order for one to learn to read standard written English, one needs receptive control of standard English. He needs to understand it when it is spoken to him or read to him. There is no reason to believe that the Black children in our urban schools cannot understand standard English (p. 24).

Citing Goodman and Baratz (1969), Sims asserts that speakers of Black English understand sentences in standard English and translate certain features into their own dialect, both orally and while reading. Goodman contends that in order for translation to occur, the readers must first arrive at the underlying meaning of the sentence. Since arriving at the meaning is the goal of reading, translation is evidence that the readers have succeeded in comprehending what they read.

Sims (1975) demonstrates that using dialect readers did not enhance children's ability to make the transition to standard material:

> An analysis of the oral reading miscues produced by a group of second graders who were reading some of the dialect-specific materials and companion stories in standard English revealed that, while the dialect did not cause any difficulty for the children, neither did it enhance the process, nor did it eliminate any problems which may have occurred in the reading of standard English (Sims, 1972). The children who were all speakers of Black dialect, were able to accomodate to either written dialect, and translated syntactic features—notable verb forms—from one dialect to the other regardless of the forms presented in the material they were using (1975, p. 24-25).

Sims deplores the content of dialect readers, noting that the authors, *looking in from the outside*, simply presented the stereotypes of the "disadvantaged" so often described in the sixties. In trying to make the characters and stories relevant to young Black readers, they have succeeded only in making the material objectionable.

Jones (1979) also centers on the question of dialect interference. Citing a study done by Piestrup (1973), his findings in part support the concept that the more Black English a child speaks, the lower his reading score will be. However, Piestrup found that

> While this general pattern held across most classroom teaching styles she found that one teaching approach was particularly effective in producing high reading achievement. The characteristics which distinguished these

classrooms (which she labeled the Black Artful Approach) were: teachers approved of Ebonics use by the students and the teachers' speech included some forms of Ebonics; teachers encouraged the child to speak, listened, did not interrupt, and responded to the child; children were enthusiastic and talked frequently; teachers used familiar words in instruction, taught meanings of familiar words and concepts, gave auditory discrimination training and used context and syntactic cues for words that sound alike in Ebonics; teachers gave correct feedback to students.

In summarizing Piestrup's research, Jones states,

> These data suggest that Ebonics per se is not an inherent barrier to reading achievement but that language awareness, as exhibited by style-switching, seems to go along with successful mastery of reading as it is traditionally taught (Jones, 1979, pp. 430-31).

Although a growing body of research supports the concept of interference, the data is not conclusive. Simons and Johnson (1974) concluded that, because dialect alone does not account for Black children's difficulties in reading, the teacher variable must be studied more closely. They found that Black children's knowledge of vocabulary corresponds well to the vocabulary of basal readers, that Black children are bi-dialectal (they can switch from Black English to standard English) and that when reading standard English a child producing Black English forms demonstrates some reading comprehension, otherwise he or she could not make that translation (Kachuck, 1978).

Shields criticizes the materials created to teach Black English speakers reading skills:

> Armed with various descriptive taxonomies of the language, conflicting statements concerning the value of Black English to Black culture, and severe negative sanction for its speakers, many self-appointed experts used information obtained from their research as the rationale for special language development projects, specifically reading instructional programs and materials, to alleviate the "Black language deficiency." Unfortunately, these efforts have turned out to be little more than stilted language drills, neutralized reading texts without cultural appeal, or Black language readers with distorted features that approximate Black characters and in some instances, reflect negative aspects of Black culture. Most significantly, they have little effect on reading acquisition (1979, p. 198).

Citing the work of Goodman and Burke (1973), Shields also focuses on the teacher variable. Noting that the researchers first embraced the interference theory and later revised their opinion, she observes

> The only special disadvantage which speakers of low-status dialects suffer in learning to read is one imposed by teachers and schools. Rejection of their dialects and educators' confusion of linguistic differences with linguistic deficiencies interfere with the natural processes by which reading is

acquired and undermines the linguistic self-confidence of divergent speakers (p.199).

Shields recommends attacking the problem through teacher self-examination, and teacher knowledge of the features of Black English so that communication is not impaired when children switch codes. She concludes that although standard English enhances school success, teachers must accept Black English as an integral part of Black culture.

Knapp (1975) echoes Shields' analysis. She points to the lack of teacher training, negative attitudes towards speech of Black English speakers, and false assumptions about the nature of nonstandard dialects, as factors causing the reading failure of Black children. She advocates a two-week inservice training course for teachers focusing on 1) identifying their attitudes toward language; 2) providing information on the systematic nature of language; 3) examining social dialects frequently stigmatized; 4) applying social dialect information to dialect interference in reading; and 5) formulating strategies capable of being implemented with a minimum of program change. She recommends the following solutions:

* accepting the child's Black English version of standard English text material
* use of the language experience approach retaining the child's syntax but using standard English spelling patterns
* using an individualized reading materials program
* using an informal reading inventory and audio tapes to assess reading levels (but not counting dialect variations as errors)

Many questions remain unanswered concerning the role that Black English should play in classrooms in which it is spoken by all or some of the students. Current educational wisdom suggests that dialect-different children have a right to speak their own language variety, as reflected by the CCCC statement of 1974. However, Lass (1978) points out that the CCCC viewpoint is generally rejected when it comes to consideration of written Black English. She notes that 1) certain researchers (Cachie, 1973; Johnson & Simons, 1973) have found that stories written in Black English are not better understood by speakers of that dialect than are stories written in standard English; 2) educators concerned with the social mobility of minorities believe that "legitimizing" Black English by using it in books encourages its use and that the result marks Blacks as uneducated, unemployable and lower-class; 3) classroom teachers are confused about how Black English texts would be used with a linguistically and racially mixed group; and 4) educators are troubled by the difficulty of committing Black English, which is primarily an oral code, to print.

Lass counters that although reading gains cannot be assured through the use of dialect materials, positive attitude changes would be a likely result of their use. She sees dialect materials as supplemental to the central reading program, and notes that Black English has been more successfully represented in children's literature than in materials written expressly to teach reading:

> In materials such as Black English basal readers (Baratz & Stewart, 1970) highly controlled vocabulary and sentence structure are substituted for real language. In literature, on the other hand, authors' voices are individualistic, thus replicating the varieties of spoken Black English (1978, p. 414).

The variety of theory and research presented in this section indicates that consensus on the issue of the relationship between Black English and reading is a distant goal. Further study in this area ought to focus on variables such as thinking and learning styles and the influence of culture on both. The next section of this paper will look at rationales for such educational programs as the Cultural Linguistic Approach, which attempts to maximize the Black child's potential for learning through culture-based methods of instruction.

Black English: What to do About it?

> . . . But he is only five years old, and doesn't yet know these words ["culturally deprived"] are meant for him. He comes to school eager to learn, excited about kindergarten. All of the people he loves in his little world have promised him by their word and deed a fantastic experience. His Uncle Joe gave him two dollars just because he was going to school. His daddy bought him new clothes to wear on his first day. His grandmama cooked a special Sunday dinner for him, and everyone came and helped him celebrate. Even his grandfather called him from Mississippi and told him all about the magic of school. Anyone who has ever been a party to this experience—teacher or parent—knows that the Black child comes to school eagerly, excitedly and ready to learn (Millender, 1980, p. 30).

The *deficit/difference* controversy of the late sixties and seventies prompted educators and linguists to prescribe a variety of methodologies and materials to "remediate" the Black child's perceived difficulties in learning to speak and read standard English. Dialect readers, "Teaching English as a Second Language" techniques and behavior modification-based reading materials are a few of the products of the Black English/reading controversy. As quickly as these programs were developed, objections to them were registered.

A significant protest came from many Black scholars who attended a national conference, held in St. Louis, Missouri in January, 1973, to discuss Black children's cognitive and language development. Critical of the work done on this subject by white researchers, Black conferees caucused among themselves to define Black language from a Black perspective. Their discussions led to the creation of the concept of *Ebonics,* which is defined as:

. . . the linguistic and paralinguistic features which on a concentric continuum represents the communicative competence of the West African, Caribbean, and United States slave descendants of African origin. It includes the various idioms, patois, argots, ideolects, and social dialects of Black people especially those who have been forced to adapt to colonial circumstances. Ebonics derives its form from ebony (black) and phonics (sound, the study of sound) and refers to the study of the language of black people in all its cultural uniqueness (Williams, 1975, p. vi).

Subsequently, these and other Black researchers have opposed isolating the language barrier issue from that of cultural difference. Citing Dillard (1972), Wofford (1979) notes that there are many minority groups who differ from the mainstream in both language and culture, the most notable group of unabsorbed persons being Black Americans:

After more than three hundred years in this country, it is clear that many of the folkways of Blacks have remained, several of them having been adopted by mainstream American culture. Even after a period of mutual influence and some narrowing of language and culture gaps, the language and culture of the majority of Blacks remains distinct from those of any large group of white Americans (p. 369).

Wofford shows that the differing phonology, grammar and lexicon of Ebonics constitutes a linguistic barrier between mainstream American and Black cultures. One of the first changes she recommends for removing the barrier is the recognition of Ebonics as a valid communication system. Equally important to breaking down the barrier, however, is the recognition that Black children's experiences do not correspond to those of middle-class American children. For example, Black children are less inclined than middle-class children to perform publicly for unfamiliar adults—particularly white adults. Black children are also not reared to volunteer information to stangers—again, particularly to white adults—because it has not proven to be advantageous. Such cultural and linguistic facts cannot be ignored in the educational processes of Black children. Critical intervention must come, says Wofford, not at the expense of debasing their cultural experiences, but rather, the procedures and materials used in the schools must be appropriate to and consistent with those cultural experiences.

Johnson (1979) also argues that the communication differences between white and Black people are understandable only in terms of cultural factors. In a recent article he compared similarities and differences of using English-as-a-second-language techniques with Ebonics speakers and foreign language speakers. He notes the "functional interference" factor, defined by Labov as the refusal to learn Mainstream American English (MAE) because it is "white folk's talk." The phenomena occurs as a result of Blacks taking increased pride in anything that is identifiably Black. Pride in their history, music, appearance, customs, and language, coupled with the reluctance of white Americans to assimilate Blacks into their culture has caused Blacks to hold on to all identity labels. Foreign language speakers do not have the functional interference problem because they do not associate the learning of English with identification with an "enemy" group or a denial of their own cultural identity.

Coupled with the issue of identity, Johnson also cites the motivational factor as a key problem faced by teachers using second language teaching techniques with Ebonics speakers. MAE is not reinforced in the children's social environment, and the segregated nature of our society has shown that Blacks who do not speak MAE have not been afforded opportunities for full participation in society. Johnson is critical of the drills used in second language teaching techniques and recommends that the students receive instruction in the nature of dialects, their causes of development, and their social implications. His most important recommendations for resolving the problem of communication differences focus on the variable of teacher training. He suggests that uppermost on educators' agendas should be teacher exposure to cultural anthropology, a field which would provide teachers with a background for understanding their students and the language they speak. Next, teachers must learn principles of linguistics—structures of language and the way the system is put together. Teachers must also be exposed to the psychology of language learning, and finally they must be re-trained in the methodology, techniques, and effective use of instructional media. Even after such measures are implemented, Johnson feels that without attacking the poverty of many students, the chances for their success (as defined by mainstream Americans) are slight.

A number of Black researchers have identified societal attitudes as a key variable in the issue of Black children and reading achievement. Following a study of an inner-city school where Black children's language *did not* interfere negatively with reading achievement, Covington (1974) poses the following questions: "What is the relationship between teachers' non-language attitudes toward their students and the students' communities, to academic achievement? In fact, are these general attitudes more powerful than specific language attitudes?" (p. 52). She concludes that language is only a small segment of the total problem: racist school systems are fostered by a racist society. Linder (1979) has reached similar conclusions:

> The basic assumption being made here is that the teaching and curriculum the Black child is exposed to do not in any way reflect his/her own experiences and culture. The current curriculum being used at the early educational level plays a major role in contributing to the process of turning Black children against themselves while, at the same time, schools view the Black child as unintelligent and continue to induce and perpetuate the

very pathology which they claim to remedy. Children who are treated as if they are educable almost invariably become educable. This is educational atrophy. It is generally known that if an arm or a leg is bound so that it cannot be used, eventually becomes unusable. The same is true of intelligence. The fact is that these children, by and large, do not learn because they are not taught effectively and they are not being taught because those who are charged with the responsibility of teaching them do not believe that they can learn, and do not expect that they can learn, and do not act toward them in ways which will help them to learn (p. 14).

Millender's (1980) analysis of the Black English controversy criticizes behavior modification readers and structured language drill programs as holdovers from the past, based on *deficit/difference* theories grounded in an atmosphere of racism and oppression. She believes that when it was no longer popular to espouse theories of Black genetic inferiority, educators borrowed from Bernstein's work to cast old theories of inferiority into a more palatable mold—"language deficiency."

Multiethnic Perspectives

The belief that cultural values should be studied, preserved, and cherished led to a new wave of "multiethnic" approaches to instruction in the 1970's. James Banks attacks instruction that is not multiethnic:

Rather than being a bridge between childhood and adult life, such education becomes a foreign no-man's land, where students are at odds with their past and unsure of their futures. Multiethnic ignorance results in the creation of Afro-Saxons or blacks who assimilate WASP views, values and behavior. Without attention to their heritage, such people become kin to Ralph Ellison's "invisible man" (Lange, 1980, p. 95).

By showing students that they are members of various groups throughout their lives and that an ethnic group is one of them, a sound multiethnic curriculum promotes greater self-understanding. Implementing a truly multiethnic perspective has been difficult. Only a few states have legislation mandating multicultural education, including California, Florida, Illinois, Iowa, Minnesota, Ohio, Pennsylvania and Wisconsin. Even when states take this step, they have generally inadequate program models to choose from. Lange (1980) has criticized what he refers to as the "additive approach," or merely adding instructional time and materials concerning individual ethnic populations while noting the accomplishments of their more famous persons. Banks is critical of this emphasis on selected heroes, for it tends to stress only the experiences of a few persons, many of whom are of questionable historical significance, rather than treating the total experiences and problems of ethnic groups from a comparative, conceptual and interdisciplinary point of view (Lange, 1980).

While not all educators have accepted even the additive approach, Banks and others have moved on to explore the deeper ramifications of cultural differences. They suggest that not only multicultural programs but bicultural programs may be appropriate for Black and Latino children whose cultural differences from the mainstream are so great as to pose specific barriers to learning. Brown notes the desirability of a bicultural approach to educational practice—"one which would develop the ability to function in the dominant culture *and* in the minority culture from which one comes"—by showing how ethnic background, value systems, and learning behaviors interact and interrelate (Lange, 1980, p. 95). In Brown's analysis, most ethnic groups adhere to a traditional value system that emphasizes group behaviors and loyalties. The educational system, however, tends toward a modernist value system that seeks to divest individuals of traditional loyalties and obligations in favor of personal freedom and fulfillment. Many culturally different students, whose cognitive styles result from cultural heritage, clash with the preferred learning styles upon which most instructional materials are based. Brown argues that being bicultural also means being bicognitive. This is a critical concept, for once it is accepted, the educator must develop a bicultural/bicognitive capacity in the students through a curriculum which focuses attention on the sociocultural characteristics of the individual learner. Such a curriculum would aim not only for inter- and intra-cultural understanding and acceptance, but also for the development of holistic social and cognitive skills in all students. Since 1969, the Cultural Linguistic Approach has developed curriculum materials and implemented an instructional program grounded in what it terms culture-based education; it therefore predates the work of Banks, Brown and others whose efforts are along similar lines. Before moving into a thorough program description, we must look at what bicultural/bicognitive—culture-based—instruction means in relationship to language and reading acquisition.

Cultural Perspectives on Language and Reading

The advent of bicultural/bicognitive educational programs had an impact on the way in which the Black English issue was viewed. By applying the bicultural/bicognitive model to language learning, linguists endorsed bidialectal and/or bilingual approaches to teaching English and reading. What distinguishes their work from the efforts of the deficit/difference practitioners is the insistence that Black English forms be accepted by educators as viable means of communication.

Schuster-Webb (1980) asserts that bidialectalsim offers the student a choice of audience and style. While standard English is the medium of school instruction, the learning of standard English can be facilitated by the teacher's awareness of dialect features spoken by her students. She notes that when a person chooses to acquire a second dialect, he must be highly motivated to embark on that learning process, for without proper motivation no attention will be paid to the learning task.

According to Schuster-Webb, this is a critical issue for it is linked to how information is processed. Cognitive psychologists have identified a system of processing where information is stored into what is called "long-term memory." Information stored in long-term memory is available for later recall, while the information the learner is not motivated to learn is often processed no further than short-term memory, to be maintained for only a brief period (up to thirty seconds), and then permanently lost from memory. Therefore, if the attitude toward the learning task is negative, then in all probability the individual will not pay attention to the information to be learned, and it will not be assimilated into long-term memory. In terms of language learning, if the student does not understand the information to be learned and cannot associate the information with anything previously learned, the information cannot be processed into long-term memory, and is thus forgotten—"in one ear and out the other." What all this means, says Schuster-Webb, is that the teacher's familiarity with Black English features can facilitate the interaction between the student and the learning task. Poetry, music, short stories and other Black English expressions can be used in the classroom in the teaching of communication skills.

Several other researchers have noted that particularly in the area of reading and language, communication difficulties could be diminished if teachers concentrated upon the goal of communicating ideas and information rather than worrying about the superficial details of style (Burling, 1973). Citing a study by Johnson and Simons (1973) on whether or not dialect readers are easier for Black children to read than standard English texts, Pietras (1979) states that the evidence showed that children did not learn better from a particular version, i.e., they could learn equally well from either. He illustrates this conclusion by showing how a Black English speaking student might read and translate a standard English passage into Black English. In this example, the child edits what is read to match his language patterns. Pietras notes that many teachers would feel that this child cannot read because he did not reproduce the words exactly as written and printed; however, he argues that a truer test of comprehension would be whether or not the child could answer questions about what he has read. Pietras concludes that the child's different language pattern is a concern for language instruction and not reading instruction. Williams and Rivers (1976) observe that this ability to translate from standard English to Black English, both in reading and oral langauge, (or "code-switching") indicates that Black children develop a great deal of cognitive ability/flexibility in order to survive in urban schools and society in general.

Granger (1976) has identified the following goal for language instruction based on the acceptance of cultural difference theories:

At present, a viable goal would be to focus on every child's ability to use whatever ideolect the child brings to the school situation in an effective manner(p. 485).

This goal is far more consistent with the changing view of the Black child. Moving from a deficit to a difference view of linguistic and cultural behavior shifts the burden for change from the child to the school. Current positive moves toward multicultural education and appreciation of cultural diversity makes the early childhood axiom of "taking the child where he or she is" more than just empty words.

In the final section of this paper the Cultural Linguistic Approach to Early Childhood Education will be described. This instructional program is one of the few programs which has successfully addressed the needs of Black English speakers as they enter the elementary school. What distinguishes this approach from others described in this paper is the program's emphasis on the student's culture as well as its unique language acquisition strategies.

The Cultural Linguistic Approach: A Key to School Success for Black Children

Perhaps the most unique aspect of Cultural Linguistics is the concept that the child is not culturally, cognitively, or linguistically deficient. It is therefore in direct theoretical contradiction to the notions that have directly and indirectly effected educational curricula, classrooms and teaching methodologies. Taking Cultural Linguistics theory a step further, the concept of "not deficient" is superseded by the concept "culturally enriched." Cultural Linguistics has been able to effectively operate a complete program of educational innovation which not only builds upon what a child brings to school, but fosters and encourages it as well (Linder, 1979).

The elementary school curriculum has to foster the social skills of living together and working together for the common good. It has to prepare young people for playing a part in the development of a society in which all members share fairly in the good or bad fortune of the group, and in which progress is measured in terms of human well-being. The demand for educational programs responsive to the needs and aspirations of America's excluded minorities is consistent with the modern American ideal of cultural pluralism. Before we can even begin to bring about equitable changes in the fabric of our society, we must first and foremost change American education.

The ideal program for a multi-cultural educational environment is one which is of instructional and social value to minority children from all ethnic backgrounds. This means that the Black child, the Mexican-American and Spanish surnamed child, the Native American child, and so on will reap benefits in line with the highest expectations of his or her community and home,as well as receive those preparatory skills needed to live in a changing world. The curriculum should inculcate a sense of commitment to the ethnic as well as to the outer community, and help students to accept the values appropriate to both worlds. Therefore, we propose that the curriculum of the public school must transmit the values of cooperative endeavor and the sharing of skills and ideas with the group. It must teach the knowledge acquired by the group. It must teach children the history and culture of their ethnic group. In addition, it must teach children the skills necessary for acquiring goods and services for the group. School studies should also give students an understanding of the organization and aims of the local as well as the larger community in order for them to negotiate both systems for the benefit of the group. The Cultural Linguistic Approach (CLA), while never purporting to be *the* solution, takes one gigantic step toward answering the demand for these quality educational materials. By its very title, Cultural Linguistics means the coordination between home (culture) and school (language—the linguistic vehicle through which values are transmitted). The development of Cultural Linguistics comes about as we continually seek new methods which join Home and School, and in particular, bring Home "back home" into our classrooms.

One of the most important factors contributing to the alienation of ethnic minority children in public schools is the rejection of the home language. Teachers who disparage the language of culturally different children endanger these children's emotional security. Many of our teachers and principals, who should know better because they see it daily, are still trying to ignore the vital role culture plays in all aspects of human endeavor. Today when the once-hazy concept of Third World peoples is an ever-present reality, American education fails to prepare the vast majority of its children to assume responsible and powerful roles in the changed world. Ignoring the omnipotence of culture and naively believing that all people are the same is, quite simply, fatal. All people are not the same. The differences in how we eat, argue, think and act must be as much a part of the curriculum in Room 222, Middleville USA as it already is in the world's marketplace.

One of the tasks undertaken by Cultural Linguistics has been a re-working of educational objectives. Many objectives designed for multi-ethnic approaches in the past have been too visionary and unrealistic. For example, goals proposed for teachers who faced culturally different children were: to become objective in self-evaluation; to overcome racial and cultural ethnocentrism; and to refrain from stereotyping (Zintz, 1969). As desirable as these goals may be, they nonetheless leave too much to a person's "willingness" to change; they leave too much to chance.

The objectives of the Cultural Linguistic Approach, on the other hand, are to change both the total classroom environment and teaching methods. The model attempts to utilize every aspect of the child's culture in a classroom situation. Through culture-based education children are motivated to learn as their school experiences become linked to themselves, their families, and their ethnic group. CLA refers to this cultural emphasis as "functional ethnicity" —content which teaches basic concepts, skills and vocabulary. Cultural content is incorporated into lessons as it relates to the content and skills being taught. The method employs a variety of resources such as pictures, ethnic objects and artifacts, historical information, cultural holidays and heroes, current events, and examples drawn from family and community experiences. Curriculum manuals developed for the program provide teachers with a wealth of cultural material to be used for skill development. The program's emphasis on functional ethnicity is at the heart of its success.

A criticism of many attempts at multicultural education lies with what has previously been referred to as the "additive approach." To simply "drop in" units on the contributions of Blacks and other ethnic groups has not provided the kind of consistent emphasis on their culture which must be present for the maximum development of ethnic minority children. Educators forget that culture is not an overcoat which the child sheds and slips into the locker before entering the classroom, only to be retrieved at the end of the day. It must be remembered that the child enters the classroom carrying culture on his back —it pervades and shapes his observations, thoughts and actions.

With this as a premise, the Cultural Linguistic Approach has developed an instructional methodology referred to by the acronym USISPU, which blends cultural content (affective domain) with skill development activities (cognitive domain) leading to skill attainment and mastery. This process for learning is one that can be adapted for use at any grade level, though it was originally developed for primary grade children.

USISPU provides the teacher with a tool for evaluating children's concept and skill attainment in each lesson. The technique is based on the concept of oral language elicitation. Though structured, it is flexible enough to be used in all subject areas. Figure 1 is a graphic representation of Cultural Linguistic Approach theory.

Explanation of Paradigm

1. *Concepts* are unlimited ideas or thoughts about phenomena. When plan-

Table 1
Cultural Linguistic Approach Learning Paradigm

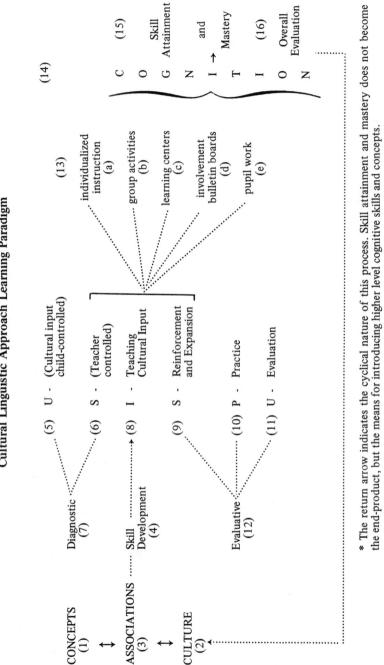

* The return arrow indicates the cyclical nature of this process. Skill attainment and mastery does not become the end-product, but the means for introducing higher level cognitive skills and concepts.

(CLA Orientation Manual, 1980, p. 7)

ning a lesson, a teacher selects some of these ideas for her presentation. This is both a conscious and a conscious selection. It is conscious because the teacher purposely chooses certain concepts to organize a specific lesson or unit. It is unconscious because a teacher's choices are always determined by her own experiences.

2. *Culture* is a way of living; it incorporates not only what a person does, but how he does it. Culture even influences the *way* a person looks at the world. Teachers should be particularly cognizant of culture because it reflects the child's conception of his environment and of who he is.

3. *Association* marries the concept and the culture. It is both a process and a skill. Association is a *process* when the teacher uses it to establish within the child a new relationship between his culture and her concept. Association becomes a *skill* when the child can incorporate the new concepts within his own cultural network. (step 9)

4. *Skill development* —at this point the teacher decides what skills are to be taught. The U and S serve as the initiators of the skill development process. During this phase of the sequence, the teacher gains some notion of what the child knows about the skills and what she should teach in order to further enhance skill development. The remainder of the sequence (I-U) focuses on developing and expanding skills.

5. *Unstructured Elicitation* is the first segment of the USISPU sequence. It is the point at which the child is allowed to freely verbalize about his understanding of a particular phenomenon. This is key because it is at this point that the child gives information about the particular stimulus introduced to him by the teacher. At the same time he gives a cultural assessment of the stimulus or phenomenon. This segment is child-centered and should be relatively free from teacher interference. The teacher should act as a listener and take note of the child's responses.

6. *Structured Elicitation* is the segment of the sequence where the teacher asks a specific question in order to determine how much the pupils know about the concept she plans to introduce. Based upon their responses, the teacher is then able to determine how her concept fits into the children's cultural network and finalize her strategy for concept presentation during her teaching.

7. *Diagnostic* —both the first unstructured and structured elicitation are defined as diagnostic. They are so defined because it is through their use that the teacher ascertains the level of understanding a child has about a particular concept and is thereby able to assess the amount of teaching needed to complete the child's understanding, if such is needed.

In addition to being diagnostic, the first Unstructured and Structured Elicitations are pre-requisite to the actual skill attainment process(Step # 14)

8. During the Interim (teaching) segment, the skill attainment process begins with the teacher's use of any or all of elements *a through e* to bring about cognition. It is important that the teacher expand not only the child's understanding of a particular concept but that she utilize culturally relevant materials to do so. Use of effective processes is key during this phase for cognitive development.

It is hoped that the teacher utilizes affective stimuli to bring about the much desired expansions in the cognitive areas.

9. *Structured Elicitation* —the second Structured Elicitation should relate directly back to the initial Structured Elicitation. This segment of the sequence serves as an indicator of the child's grasp of a particular concept. If the teacher is not satisfied at this point with the child's progress, she may go into the practice session for additional reinforcement or, if necessary, return to the Interim phase to re-teach. This segment is therefore evaluative in nature.

10. *Practice* —this segment of sequence is used by the teacher to reinforce and expand teachings from the *Interim* lesson. Practice could incorporate elements a - e as well.

11. *Unstructured Elicitation* —this is the final segment of the sequence, and thereby should complete the cognitive process, but only in the sense that it signals the child's attainment of specific skills. The optimum goal of the final Unstructured Elicitation is to have the child utilize association as a skill. As such, the child will indicate an incorporation of the new concept within his own cultural network. The teacher will be able to assess this process if the child indicates by his response a synthesis of material introduced during the interim lesson.

12. *Evaluative* —both the second *Unstructured* and *Structured Elicitation* are defined as *Evaluative*. They are so defined because at this point the teacher can evaluate the level of concept attainment.

13. *Elements a through e* will occur primarily in the Interim phase and afterwards. However, an element such as *d* will often occur as an outgrowth of the final *U* and may be used as the beginning of a whole unit.

14. *Cognition* is understanding. It rightly looms over the entire USISPU sequence because the overall goal of USISPU is to bring about understanding. Understanding, then, is not the end but the beginning of knowledge. While cognition is the goal, affective stimuli are the central vehicles for cognitive development.

15. *Skill Attainment* and *Mastery* which begins in the diagnostic phase of USISPU climaxes here. The teacher should be able to identify the progress of Skill Attainment in a particular area; *Mastery* should be ascertainable

from the child's use of the skill in many situations. It is therefore essential that the teacher provide many opportunities for the child to apply skills taught.

16. *Overall Evaluation* —overall evaluation of children's progress, concept and skill development take place after Skill Attainment and Mastery of the concept(s). It includes future lesson development and planning, administering of manual mastery and achievement tests as well as data collection by the teacher and school (CLA Orientation Manual, 1980, pp. 8-9).

The schools place tremendous importance on the teaching of language arts. Where many schools fail, however, is in insisting that all children learn the same language in the same way at the same time. The dangers of such a tendency—grounded in the "melting pot" theory—are slowly being challenged by culture-based curriculum and methodology.

The Cultural Linguistic Approach has stood firm in the midst of the recent furor over the acceptance of Black English in our nation's public schools. CLA rejects the notion that the culture or spoken language of low-income Black children is in any way deficient or inferior compared to other ethnic language styles or cultural expressions. Throughout its history, CLA has attempted to re-teach those who have been led to believe that Black culture nurtures inferiority or that Black language expresses sub-standard utterances of a deficient people.

The Cultural Linguistic Approach to language development is both extensive and substantive. It is concerned more with how well a child communicates than with how he talks. The program places emphasis not only on vocabulary enrichment, but on sentence expansion, role-demanding language, cognitive demands of language, topic, context, situation, fluency, appropriate time and place, clarity, precision and foresight as well. It is vitally important that schools prepare children with these skills so they may take their rightful places in society. The goal of the CLA language development program is the growth and development of the communicative ability of the child. The child is taught to *use* his langauge ability to learn independently, inquire intelligently and to think creatively.

Black and other inner-city children come to school with a conceptual foundation rooted in their own language capabilities. Upon arriving, the process of destroying their language system begins. The foundation for concept building is thereupon blocked. They continue to build concepts outside of school that do not require them to use a language which denies this already acquired foundation. Black children manipulate rhythms, intonation, gestures and rhyme in their communicative acts. They can vary both rhythm and intonation in a way that varies the meaning of a sentence. Children are able to carry on lengthy exchanges of in-house mockery with the sole aim of out-scoring each other's verbal abilities.

The confusion arises when teachers equate labeling with conceptualization. Employing a different word or no word at all, does not indicate the absence of a concept. Children may use an entirely different word order (grammar) unfamiliar to the teacher, who may falsely conclude that they have not acquired the concept. It is as necessary to convince children that what they already know is important, respected and usable, as it is to convince the people who teach them (CLA Orientation Manual, KG-PI, 1974, p. 1).

When the question of "correcting" Black language arises, many teachers' attitudes range from indifferent to hysterical. The Cultural Linguistic Approach asks that teachers refrain from "tampering" with the child's language because, linguistically, there is no right or wrong language. Many teachers using the Approach invariably ask, "I know we aren't supposed to 'correct' the children, but when do we teach them what's 'right'?" The illogic of such a statement, if not apparent on a superficial level, certainly is revealed when one looks beyond the surface.

Teachers who hammer into students' heads "he is, they are," and so on at the expense of teaching the language of mathematics, science, economics or the social sciences, are among the major contributors to the closed doors these students will face in the "open" job market. Inadequate and unrealistic job preparation, combined with the lip service paid to developing the minds of youth, help give a "shot-in-the-arm" to institutional racism in employment.

Teachers who still doubt the legitimacy of Black language and who have the need to "correct" their pupils should ask themselves, "What will I correct? In my efforts to alter a specific pupil's response, am I making the child a more effective (not socially-acceptable) speaker? Do I know enough about the nature of language and language learning to "tamper" with the child's speech? Do I concentrate too much on how well a child speaks? Have I concentrated on the development of thinking skills in my students?" The CLA initially developed its oral language manual curriculum guides so that teachers could begin to put CLA theory and USISPU methodology into practice. These manuals served as the prototype for curriculum manuals in social studies, science and mathematics.

The Cultural Linguistic Approach Oral Language Manual

The CLA Oral Language Manual is developed according to culture-based dictates. Its instructions are based on these social, psychological and linguistic theories:

* The child's language represents the norm of his family and community.

* If a child can express a concept in his first language, he possesses the concept.

* The teacher must provide as realistic a context for language experiences as possible using materials from the child's culture.

* The pupil's self-identity must be supported at all times.

* The Black language system is a complete, well-ordered language system; it has a phonology, a lexicon, and a grammar, as well as non-verbal elements.

* The child will continue to speak his primary language system.

CLA divides language arts curriculum into three broad categories: descriptive vocabulary, cognitive vocabulary and expressive vocabulary. The manual focuses on these broad areas, providing units with concepts, performance objectives and sample USISPU lessons for each category.

Section I concentrates on the descriptive vocabulary so basic to expressing ideas. Many of the units focus on assigning labels for familiar objects and concepts. Armed with a descriptive vocabulary, children can begin to share their thoughts and ideas with others in their environment.

Section II concentrates on the language of thought, and contains units designed to strengthen the child's instructional vocabulary. Each unit builds a progression that follows the steps in problem-solving. Lessons in this section are designed to sharpen critical thinking skills and to train youngsters to use problem-solving techniques as they strive for peaceful coexistence with their environment.

Section III focuses on the expressive (creative)process of communications. Units and lessons are designed to help the child explore and express his inner feelings, and to learn a variety of ways to convey thoughts and emotions. This section begins with a unit on the physical, sensory and emotional aspects of the self. From there children expand their expressive vocabularies through role-playing, story-telling, and finally through evaluation and judgment, which represents the highest order of the thought process.

The CLA Oral Language Manual is designed to show teachers how to develop conceptual understandings in children through the use of oral language. Four grade levels have been developed: Kindergarten, Primary I, Primary II, and Primary III. On all levels, the manuals focus on cognitive skill development and include the following:

1) observation
2) labeling
3) classification
4) association
5) cause and effect linkage
6) sequence and ordering
7) conclusion and inference
8) evaluation

Though content varies according to grade level, each student is provided maximum opportunities to use his oral language to describe, explain, question, entertain, teach and solve problems using visual aids and experiences as culturally relevant to him as possible.

The Cultural Linguistic Approach's Reading Program

Recent reseach suggests that practice in oral expression has a more positive effect on beginning reading than does dialect training. Beginning reading materials center on finding out what kind of material can best enable children to build on the language strengths they bring to school. The language and experiences children bring to the classroom can provide a foundation on which all areas of instruction—not only reading—is based. It is well-documented that oral language proficiency facilitates learning to read. New evidence indicates that young children's growing consciousness of oral and written language is also a factor in their success in learning to read. Research on linguistic awareness suggests that the importance of oral language development as a foundation for learning to read cannot be overstated. Oral language fluency not only provides speaking and listening skills which have direct counterparts in reading and writing, but also provides linguistic access to grammatical structures needed for reading with understanding.

This is not to suggest that young children receive direct instruction in specific linguistic variables such as syntactic awareness or word consciousness, but rather, that linguistic awareness is facilitated in young children by providing a natural language environment in which oral and written language are used as communication tools.

Combined with the CLA Oral Language program, the language experience approach is a key component of what CLA views as a balanced approach to teaching reading. Through the language-experience approach, the communication skills of speaking, listening and writing are brought together for the child. Drawing on a vast network of cultural experiences, the young Black child is able to see and read about his own thoughts and experiences and share them with his classmates. His words and experiences become valued as they are recorded on charts and paper. The motivation for learning to read is intensified. Along with this approach, CLA recommends the use of good literature, culturally relevant instructional materials and continuous opportunities for language practice. These features, coupled with the teacher's own or a commercial reading series provide the balance for Black and other ethnic minority children to achieve reading success.

Cultural Linguistic Approach Implementation

The Cultural Linguistic Approach was developed in 1969 at Northwestern Illinois University's Center for Inner City Studies. Funded by the Department of Education's Follow Through Division, the program operates in the Chicago, Illinois and Topeka, Kansas public schools. Pupils in the program are predominantly Black, with some Mexican-Americans and Native Americans in the Topeka program. The program has also operated in Compton California and Akron, Ohio. Since the program's inception, 20,000 children and their families have been served in the public sector, and 650 teachers, paraprofessionals and administrators have been trained. Through participation in workshops and conferences, Cultural Linguistic Approach theory and methodology has reached 250 teachers and 3,000 children in alternative school settings.

CLA staff have developed a variety of instructional materials to supplement their curriculum manuals. The staff monitors program implementation in the schools at regular intervals and provides on-going staff development for all program teachers, aides, and administrators. Initially the majority of teacher training focused on language acquisition and development, features of Black language, principles of linguistics, and sociological theory. With this firm foundation, the teaching staff's attitude toward and understanding of culturally different children was broadened sufficiently for them to implement the program with the proper philosophical perspective. To be successful, any program must have the support and approval of those who are entrusted to carry it out.

Program evaluation consists of model-specific monitoring instruments as well as standardized achievement tests. Data from recent evaluations clearly demonstrate that students in the Cultural Linguistic Approach exhibit significant gains in reading compared to control-group children in pre- and post-test designs (Pentecoste, 1979).

While the educational community still argues about the issue of Black English, few programs have successfully developed a theory and method for teaching the Black child. The Cultural Linguistic Approach holds promise for addressing the heretofore largely unmet needs of America's Black children. Unfortunately, programs like CLA can only partially solve the problem of educating Black children in this country. As long as racism undergirds educational and other insititutions in this country, the issue of the Black child's language only serves to camouflage what is really happening to Black children. The concern for teaching standard English has served to de-emphasize teaching Black children the skills they will need to survive as adults. Yes, the Black child needs control of the language. His need is to extend his control of English so that he has a command of all levels of that language and can use whatever kind of English a given situation calls for—the position taken in teaching other American students. If we lose track of this point, countless more Black children will pass through the school doors without receiving the kind of education they need to function successfully in the real world. We must consider Naomi Millender's words and ask ourselves the question she poses:

And even today, in 1979, we are still looking at the Black child and his family as if they were some kind of criminals. We, meaning Blacks in the "know," are still advocating out-moded and insane techniques to "better help Black children" while other children are steady learning real skills for a real world. What difference does it make whether a Black child no longer uses "ain't" in his job interview when he ain't got nothing to offer the employer?! Who cares about mainstream or standard English when this child knows nothing about the English used in math, science or technology? Who can really afford to care about whether Black language is used in school reading materials when neither language addresses itself to the harsh realities our children face every minute of their lives? And while we argue about the "legitimacy" or "illegitimacy" or Black language, the beat goes on. Other children are learning to take their rightful places in the new America even when they speak an Italian, or German, or Greek, or Polish version of English, as well as other languages entirely, like Spanish. But our children hang in limbo while we try to make up our minds about the obvious. There's no question about our legitimacy. Our language and our culture are okay. But are we (1980, p. 34)?

REFERENCES

Baldwin, J. If Black English isn't a language, then tell me, what is? *New York Times,* Sunday July 29, 1979, E19.

Bernstein, Basil. Social class and linguistic development: A theory of social learning. In A.H. Halsey, J. Floud & C. Anderson (Eds.), *Education, Economics and Society.* New York: Free Press, 1961.

Black, M.H. Characteristics of the culturally disadvantaged child. *Reading Teacher,* 1965, *18,* 465-470.

Brown, T.J. & Taylor, O. Should Black English be taught in the elementary schools: Point/ counterpoint. *Instructor,* 1980, *89,* 22.

Burling, R. *English in Black and white.* New York: Holt, Rinehart & Winston, Inc., 1973.

Cachie, Grace.   The Effect of Two Language Experience Approaches on the Reading Comprehension, Visual Discrimination, and Work Knowledge Performance of Black Kindergarten Students Who Are Speakers of Nonstandard Dialects. Ph. D. dissertation, New York University, 1973.

Center for Inner City Studies. *Cultural linguistic approach follow through program proposal 1980-81,* Chicago: Center for Inner City Studies, 1979.

Center for Inner City Studies. *Cultural linguistic approach language position paper.* Chicago: Center for Inner City Studies, 1979.

Center for Inner City Studies. *Cultural linguistic approach oral language manual kindergarten-primary I.* Chicago: Center for Inner City Studies, 1974.

Corbett, E.P.J. (Ed.), *College composition and communicaiton.* Urbana, Illinois: National Council of Teachers of English, 1974.

Covington, A. Teachers' attitudes toward Black English. In Robert L. Williams (Ed.), *Ebonics: The true language of Black folks*. St. Louis: Institute of Black Studies, 1974.

Deutsch, M. The disadvantaged child and the learning process. In A.H. Passow (Ed.), *Education in depressed areas*. New York: Teachers College Press, 1963.

Dillard, J.L. *Black English*. New York: Randon House, 1972.

Dillingofski, M.S. Sociolinguistics and reading: A review of the literature. *The Reading Teacher*, 1979, *33* (4) 307-12.

DuBois, B. The social dialect controversy and the teaching of reading. *Reading Improvement*, 1979, *14* (4) 294-98.

Engelmann, S. How to construct effective language programs for the poverty child. In F. Williams, (Ed.), *Language and poverty*. Chicago: Markham, 1970.

Goodman, K.S. & Buck, C. Dialect barriers to reading comprehension revisited. *The Reading Teacher*, 1973, *27*, 6-12.

------------. Study of children's behavior while reading orally. *Final Report*, March, 1968. U.S. Department of Health, Education and Welfare, Office of Education, Contract Number OE 6-10-136.

Granger, R.C. The non-standard speaking child: Myths past and present. *Young Children*, 1976, *31*, 479-85.

Jensen, Arthur. How much can we boost IQ and scholastic achievement? *Harvard Educational Review*, 1969.

Johnson, K. Teaching mainstream American English: Similarities and differences with speakers of Ebonics and speakers of foreign languages. *Journal of Black Studies*, 1979, *9* (4), 411-22.

Johnson, Kenneth R. and Simons, Herbert D. Black children's reading of dialect and standard tests: A final report. ED 176 978 April, 1973.

Joiner, C.W. Memorandum opinion and order: *Martin Luther King Junior Elementary School Children et al. v. Ann Arbor School District Board, 473 F. Supp. 1371* [1979].

Jones, C. Ebonics and reading. *Journal of Black Studies*, 1979, *9*, 423-48.

Kachuck, B. Black English and reading: Reading issues. *Education and Urban Society*, 1978, *10*, 385-98.

Knapp, M.O. Black dialect and reading: What teachers need to know. *Journal of Reading*, 1975, *19*, 231-36.

Lange, B. Multiethnic dimensions in English. *English Journal*, 1980, *69* (4), 95-98.

Lass, B. Review of *Bridge: A cross-culture reading program*. *Journal of Reading*, 1978, *27*, 760-61.

Linder, D.R. Viewpoint: An era of change. . . a time of transition . . . some thoughts to think about. *Black Child Journal*, 1979, *1* (1).

McHenry, D. Words of the week. *Jet*, 1980, *57* (25), 40.

Monteith, M. Black English and the reading teacher. *Journal of Reading*, 1980, *23*, 556-59.

Millender, N. They're okay: Are you? *Black Child Journal*, 1980, *1* (2), 30-35.

Nurss, J.R. Linguistic awareness and learning to read. *Young Children*, 1980, *35* (3), 57-66.

Nuru, N. Black English: Who be a winner? *Black Child Journal*, 1980, *1* (3), 14-20.

Pentecoste, J.C. *Cultural linguistic approach evaluation report 1979-80*. Chicago: Center for Inner City Studies, 1980.

Piestrup, A. *Black dialect interference and accomodation of reading instruction in first grade*. Berkeley, California: Language Behavioral Research Laboratory, 1973.

Pietras, T.P. Teaching as a linguistic process in a cultural setting. *The Clearinghouse*, 1979, *53* (4), 165-68.

Rasberry, W. Black English sensitivity. *Chicago Tribune,* July 17, 1979, sec. 3, p. 3.

Rowan, C.T. Black English is silly. *Chicago Sun-Times,* July 10, 1979, p. 36.

Schuster-Webb, K. The case for Black English revisitied. *Viewpoints in Teaching and Learning,* 1980, *56* (1), 88-95.

Seymour, C.M. and Seymour, H.N. The symbolism of Ebonics: I'd rather switch than fight. *Journal of Black Studies,* 1979, *9* (4), 397-410.

Shields, H. The language of poor Black children and reading performance. *Journal of Negro Education,* 1979, *48* (2) 196-208.

Simons, H.D. and Johnson, K.R. Black English syntax and reading interference. *Research in the Teaching of English,* 1974, *8,* 339-58.

Simpkins, G., Holt, G. and Simpkins, C. *Bridge: A cross-culture reading program.* Boston: Houghton-Mifflin Co., 1977.

Sims, R. Black children and the language arts. In Robert L. Williams (Ed.), *Ebonics: The true language of Black folks.* St. Louis: Institute of Black Studies, 1975, 22-27.

Williams, Robert L. (Ed.), *Ebonics: The true language of Black folks.* St. Louis: Institute of Black Studies, 1975.

Williams, R. & Rivers, W. Mismatches in testing. Paper read at the Conference on Testing, Washington, D.C., 1976.

Wofford, J. Ebonics: A legitimate system of oral communication. *Journal of Black Studies,* 1979, *9* (4), 367-82.

Wolfram, Walt. The relationship of white southern speech to vernacular Black Egnlish. *Language,* 1974, *50,* 498-527.

------------. *A sociolinguistic description of Detroit Negro speech.* Arlington, Virginia: Center for Applied Linguistics, 1969.

Zintz, M.V. *Education across culture.* Dubuque, Iowa: Kedell and Hunt Publishing Co., 1969.

BLACK ENGLISH: AN AGENDA FOR THE 1980's

Orlando L. Taylor

Dr. Taylor is a Professor of Communication in the Department of Communication, Arts and Sciences, at Howard University in Washington, D.C. He served as chairman of the department from 1975 to 1980. Dr. Taylor has been involved in extensive research and program development in the areas of dialect and reading, and is widely published. He is currently the Secretary of the World Congress on Black Communication.

In a recent article on a completely different topic, I began by recalling Dionne Warwick's hit record, *Deja Vu*. I am reminded of both the record and the article as I attempt to summarize the proceedings at the NIE-Ann Arbor Conference on Black English and place them in perspective. It is a matter of record that most, if not all, of the issues addressed at the conference have been addressed—and debated—for almost two decades. In summary, these issues focus on questions of the following types:

* Is there such a thing as Black English?

* If so, what are its characteristics?

* Where did it come from?

* How has it been influenced by other English dialects, as well as other languages of the world?

* Who speaks it?

* Where and when is it spoken?

* What are the prevailing attitudes toward it, and how are these attitudes manifested educationally, economically, and socially?

* How should speakers of Black English be assessed?

* What are the educational implications for speakers of Black English with respect to educational diagnoses, school placement, curriculum development (especially in the language arts), classroom materials, etc.?

This feeling of having been here before should not be construed as a criticism of the conference, nor the need for it. Quite the contrary. Spurred on by the "Ann Arbor Black English Decision," which placed many of the above issues into a *legal*, as well as an educational paradigm, interest in and discussion of Black American language and communicative behaviors—and what, if anything, to do about them—have heightened immensely. Equally important, there has been increased recognition of the need for these topics to be approached from the perspective of the needs, wishes, and rights of Black children, Black parents, and Black communities.

Thus, the Ann Arbor Black English litigation was quite timely. It occurred at a time when scholarship in the area of Black English was beginning to wane, despite the fact that clear and definitive data-based answers were generally unavailable for most of the issues raised above. Interestingly, the re-emergence of Black English as a prominent subject of inquiry in the linguistic sciences has been stimulated by parents, and not by scholars. For this reason, Black English is no longer an esoteric subject discussed by linguists, anthropologists, and a few educators alone. Because of the Ann Arbor case, I suspect that Black families and communities will assume stronger roles in future research and educational programs for Black English speakers.

The following major issues were discussed at the NIE-Ann Arbor Conference on Black English. They are presented here along with a few suggestions about where we should go from here—and why!

Community Involvement

Papers and discussions at the Ann Arbor Conference, taken in the context of the aforementioned litigation, reaffirmed a need for community involvement in deliberations on the subject of Black American speech. The proceedings clearly suggested a need for future discussion and action on this subject to include a cross-section of Black community members reflective of various social, economic, educational, and occupational sub-groups. This orientation permeated the NIE-Ann Arbor conference and is likely to greatly influence future scholarship and educational programming on this topic.

Comprehensive Definitions

Definitions of "Black English" are in need of serious re-thinking and refinement. Scholars have obviously erred in defining Black English as a nonstandard variety of English exclusively, and in implying that vernacular forms of language are spoken primarily, if not exclusively, by lower-class, nonstandard speakers. Why, for instance, is Black English Vernacular always compared to Standard English, rather than to Standard English Vernacular?

Inadequate definitions have resulted in the inaccurate protrayal of many Black speakers who, though clearly demonstrating ethnicity in their speech, nonetheless do not strictly conform to prevailing definitions. For example, current definitions do not account for middle-class Black speakers who use Standard English phonology and grammar when speaking informally, while simultaneously using Black rhetorical style, prosodic features, and idioms. This linguistic profile is not compatible with Black English Vernacular, certainly not the type typically defined in the literature. Conversely, it is a bit absurd to argue that when a Black speaker uses Standard English grammar and phonology he or she is no longer Black.

If Standard English is always defined as being either white English or even American English, then Black English by inference must clearly be nonstandard. Many Black students implicitly accept this myth by perceiving the acquisition of standard English as a rejection of their Blackness. As Ora Simpson pointed out in her paper,[*] however, standard English can be taught from a community perspective which preserves both Standard and nonstandard forms by specifying the situations where each can be used. Interestingly, this notion is not really new. Standard English has been taught for decades in different regions of the United States in such a way as to preserve local dialects. In such cases, Standard English instruction typically focuses on uniformity in grammatical rules, while permitting regional variations in such dimensions of language as phonology, idiom, vocabulary, slang, prosody, pragmatics, narrative style, non-verbal acts, and so on.

Future researchers, theoreticians, and practitioners might well begin to redefine Black American English from a far more comprehensive model rather than from ones which highlight the most extreme and exotic cases of Black verbal behavior. While current models may be defended on the grounds that they focus on the most stigmatized and penalized forms of Black speech, they, nonetheless, lead to a type of negative linguistic stereotyping.

Many points raised at the conference offer clear directions for new definitions. For instance, Labov, echoing a position taken by Taylor as early as 1974, suggested that future definitions of Black speech behavior should focus on the totality of communicative behaviors in Black communities, rather than on an isolated set used by a small segment of these communities. If this notion is adhered to, then it is clear that any comprehensive definition should take at least three factors into account.

First, Black American speech, like the speech of any socially identifiable group in the world, varies as a function of the concurrence and interaction of

---

[*] [Simpson's paper does not appear in this volume —Ed.]

several social and cultural factors, chief among them being: (a) socio-eco-nomic status, (b) region, (c) age, (d) gender, and (e) education. Thus, the de-finition of Black English should be sufficiently broad to accurately describe, for example, Gullah speakers in South Carolina, Jamaican speakers in New York City, and Black bourgeoisie speakers in Washington, D.C.

Second, definitions of Black English should reflect recognition of the fact that no language or dialect exists as a totally isolated phenomenon. Features of language and dialects typically overlap for a number of political, social, economic, and educational reasons. Even in Standard English, where many variations exist, there are marked similarities with other American English dia-lects, notably Southern white English (Underwood's point). But there are also numerous similarities among the varieties of Black speech spoken in the Unit-ed States and, in many cases, around the world. Taylor(1974)has discussed in-ter- and intra-group overlaps of Black American English, including the variety he calls "Standard Black English." It is very likely that these overlaps result from multi-dimensional influences of various languages and dialects upon each other.

Finally, a comprehensive view of Black English should take into account cultural dimensions of Black cognition and world view, together with their overlaps with other systems of thought and ways of viewing reality. The point here is that language, both verbal and non-verbal, is a symbolic system repre-sentative of the concepts of speakers in a given society. These concepts, like the symbols themselves, are influenced by the concurrence of the same social and cultural factors listed above. Because of this intimate interaction between culture, language, and cognition, any comprehensive definition of Black En-glish must take each of these factors into account. It is because of this inter-action that Black speakers often attach different meanings to words used by European speakers. The mapping of the cognitive dimension on to language is illustrated nicely in the African view of time revealed in markers of tense, mood, and aspect in Black English as discussed in Labov's paper. Diop (1978) also provides an excellent discussion of the African view of reality.

A Communication vs. A Linguistic Model

Black English is typically viewed as a collection of phonological, semantic, and grammatical rules. In other words, it is usually placed within a classical linguistic framework. Because participants at the NIE-Ann Arbor conference came from a number of academic disciplines, including many sub-specialties within the language and communication arts and sciences, one could not help but recognize the inadequacy of viewing the language of Blacks—or any other group—from the relatively narrow orientation of linguistics. What appears to be needed is a *communication*, not a *linguistic*, model to adequately address issues related to Black English.

On careful examination, the need for a communication model ought to be obvious. For descriptive purposes, we know that a language is more than a dictionary of words, sentences and sounds. Advances in pragmatics, if nothing else, tell us that language is a social tool which links utterances to specified social intentions—a phenomenon analyzed by means of the speech act. Further, we know that one must be able to use appropriate conversational rules, narrative styles, rhetorical devices, non-verbal behaviors, vocal characteristics, and so on as a function of social situations.Hall makes this point eloquently in his paper[*] by asserting that the vernacular/formal dimension is far too simplistic for describing the wide range of social situations in which one is expected to be "competent" in order to be considered an effective user of language.

It might therefore be argued that future discussions of theory, definition, and education relative to Black English should be couched in a communication competence model. In this connection, communication competence is defined as "the speaker-listener's knowledge not only of what is grammatically correct, but of what is socially appropriate and acceptable" (Bell, 1976). This notion has already been adopted by many of the successful and culturally sensitive programs which attempt to teach the language of education to Black children while simultaneously encouraging the preservation of community communicative behaviors.

At the NIE-Ann Arbor conference, the language arts programs described by Simpson in the Dallas Independent School District (Rational Black English), Perry of the San Diego City Schools, and Starks at the Center for Inner City Studies in Chicago (the Affective Domain of Language) reflect communicative competence orientations. Lewis, Hoover, and their colleagues began to develop language arts programs with this orientation as far back as the early 1970's in East Palo Alto, California. In all of these programs, notions such as bidialectalism and code-switching are handled easily. More importantly, the concept of communicative competence should help to remove, or at least reduce, the conflicts many Black students face when given the choice of speaking Standard English or Black English.

Development of Culturally Fair Tests for Black English Speakers

Tests of various types permeate American life generally, and schools in particular.   Virtually   all tests in current use in the United States use Stan-

---

* [Hall's paper does not appear in this volume —Ed.]

dard English as the medium, and sometimes the subject, of assessment. This phenomenon represents a *prima facie* case of bias against speakers of most varieties of Black English, with the possible exception of Standard Black English. (Of course, there are other sources of test bias based on such variables as region, social class, and gender.) Hoover, Politzer and Taylor (1975) have written a comprehensive treatise on this subject, using diagnostic reading tests to demonstrate sources of bias in standardized tests against speakers of Black English.

The issue of test bias was a subject of discussion at the NIE-Ann Arbor conference. Most participants agreed that Black parents and the Black community want to know that their children are progressing in school, and that data are needed to evaluate teachers' performance. At the same time, there was little question that assessment procedures must be culturally and linguistically appropriate for the test-takers. This position is buttressed by several recent legal rulings and legislative actions which make non-discriminatory testing an aspect of one's civil rights.

Implementation of a non-discriminatory testing program for Black English speakers is not a simple matter. As Hall stated in his paper, non-discriminatory testing does not necessarily result from a translation of traditional Standard English tests into Black English. Not only are there some cognitive elements which appear to be unique to Black speakers, but more importantly, there are dimensions of language not assessed in typical tests which are likely to be particularly sensitive to many aspects of Black communicative behavior, e.g., pragmatics. Assessment is also complicated by variations *within* Black English.

Research on non-discriminatory testing in the next few years might well focus on determining fair methods for addressing the following topics:

(a) the social situation of testing
(b) test directions
(c) cognitive bases of items
(d) values inherent in items
(e) language expectation of items
(f) scoring of items
(g) subject population for item analysis, selection and standardization

Defining School and Community Goals on Language

For more than two decades, a debate has raged on over language goals for the Black English speaker. Positions advanced have included: (a) teaching in Black English, (b) teaching Standard English without regard to Black English, and (c) teaching Standard English by utilizing and encouraging Black English. All too often, philosophies relative to teaching the Black child have been determined almost exclusively by scholars and professional educators. The Ann Arbor Black English case will, in all likelihood, change that situation. In that litigation, the plaintiffs argued, in effect, that while they wanted their children to learn the language of education, they also wanted the instructional process to take the language of the home and the community into account. This position is consistent with the results of Taylor's (1974) and Hoover's (1978) nationwide surveys of Black parents' langauge attitudes and expectations.

One major need of the future is a clear articulation of school language policy with regard to all members of school and general communities. All too often, these policies are not clearly communicated. The result is confusion, unnecessary suspicions, and inconsistent language policies differing from teacher to teacher and school to school. One of the attractive features of both the Dallas and San Diego programs described in these proceedings is that they clearly enunciate language policies constructed with community input. These programs also contain vigorous public relations components and educational campaigns designed to "sell" the policy to professional, general, and Black communities. More developments of this type should occur in the 1980's in other communities throughout the country.

Culturally Oriented Curriculum and Instructional Strategies

Once acceptable educational philosophies and goals have been established for Black English speakers, culturally oriented curriculum and instructional strategies must be developed. Both the curriculum and the strategies should be based on linguistic characteristics of various types of Black English. They should also reflect sensitivity to, (a) cultural and cognitive dimensions of various aspects of Black culture, (b) principles of second dialect instruction, and (c) learning styles of Black children (Cobbs & Winokur, 1977). Presumably, the language arts curriculum will be designed to teach Black students to read, speak, write and auditorily comprehend the language of education (including regional varieties of Black Standard English), while preserving vernacular forms of local Black communities. The San Diego and Dallas language arts programs reflect these sensitivities and goals.

Classroom materials for Black English speakers should also reflect cultural and linguistic sensitivity. Developers of these materials must be extremely cautious lest they run the risk of alienating Black parents and community leaders. This fate has befallen many noble efforts in the past. The problem is that such materials are typically perceived as devices to *teach* Black English, rather than to teach the language of education by taking into account the native linguistic behaviors of the learners. One way to resolve problems of this type would be to involve parents and community people in the materials development process, and to organize vigorous educational/public relations campaigns to "sell" the materials to parents, students, teachers, and community leaders.

Research on materials development should be extremely useful to the development of a theory of second dialect learning and instruction. To date, most theories on the learning of second language systems have been based on the bilingual rather than the bidialectal situation. Data on teaching the language arts to Black English speakers could contribute substantially to developing theories and materials for teaching speakers other English dialects.

Attitudes and Black English

Negative attitudes toward nonstandard dialects generally, and toward Black English in particular, have been the topic of considerable research in sociolinguistics. Some scholars have argued that negative language attitudes, especially by teachers, are a major cause for poor academic performance of Black students in reading and the other language arts. The Ann Arbor Black English decision has cast this position into a legal perspective. Judge Joiner's ruling implies that teacher's attitudes, as revealed by their lack of awareness of Black English and their subsequent failure to take Black English into account in the instructional process, are a major cause of reading failures among Black students.

While an intriguing and certainly tenable position, there is still insufficient data to accept the attitude hypothesis unequivocally. To be sure, a considerable amount of data have been generated on attitudes toward Black English. Yet, a number of questions still remain. Until the data base is complete, it could be dangerous to overstate the attitude case. If programs based on the thesis fail, considerable ammunition will have been given to individuals who resist sociolinguistic approaches to language arts education.

To date, research on attitudes toward Black English has focused primarily on teachers' attitudes, although there has been some study of students' and parents' attitudes. Major research on this topic includes the work of Taylor (1973) and Politzer and his colleagues (Politzer & Hoover, 1976, 1977; Politzer & Lewis, 1978; Politzer, 1979). This research has revealed a wide range of attitudes towards Black English, ranging from very negative to very positive to uncertain. In general, positive attitudes are professed by teachers toward more standard varieties of Black English. Culturally aware teachers tend to profess the most positive attitudes toward vernacular varieties of Black speech. Students, by contrast, have revealed far more positive attitudes toward vernacular Black speech than their parents and teachers.

Despite the existence of a body of knowledge on language attitudes, many important questions remain unanswered. Chief among them involves the appropriate   methodology to validly assess the attitudes of subjects; that is, how to distinguish between what people profess verbally and what they truly believe and feel. Most studies on this topic have required subjects either to label or categorize various speech forms, or to indicate their relative agreement and disagreement with various statements about language and language use. What is needed, however, is the development of commitment type scales to assess language attitudes. Such scales would focus on what individuals are willing to *do* based on their attitudes. For example, it is one thing to say that you respect Black English as a language form, and quite another to be willing to develop an instructional program based on a respect for Black English or to hire a person who speaks Black English.

Future research on language attitudes might explore various dimensions of language attitudes. Attitudes toward language, or anything else, are rarely unidimensional. For instance, one might have a very positive attitude toward the structure of Black English and its worth to Black people and the Black community, while simultaneously holding negative attitudes toward educational programs which utilize Black English as a medium of instruction. Future research might focus more on the language attitudes of Black parents, community leaders, and students, in addition to teachers.

A far more serious need exists to research the likely effects of positive attitude changes on educational practice and ultimately, on students' achievement in the language arts. An underlying assumption of the Ann Arbor Black English decision is that more knowledge about Black English and more positive attitudes toward it will lead to more effective institutional programs for teaching reading and other language skills to Black English speakers. This assumption, while tenable, has not been confirmed totally by data, although the work of Covington (1974), Politzer & Hoover (1977), Politzer & Lewis (1978) and Politzer (1979) suggest some correlation between teachers' language attitudes and student performance.

Although interesting, the language attitude change hypothesis, taken in isolation, is probably a simplistic view of language education for the Black English speaker. The point is that while it is reasonable to postulate that positive language attitudes are pre-requisites for effective language arts education, it is, nonetheless, highly unlikely that positive attitudes alone will result in increased academic achievement. They are likely, however, to stimulate the development of culturally and linguistically sensitive educational policies.

International and Interdisciplinary Involvement

Two facts are clear from the NIE-Ann Arbor conference on Black English. First, no single discipline in the langugage sciences has the capacity to answer *all* of the questions relative to the topic of Black English. To be sure, the discipline of linguistics is essential. However, disciplines such as anthropology, sociology, education, psychology, and speech communication can clearly contribute to our understanding of Black English, and to the development of effective, humane approaches to teaching reading and language to Black English speakers.

The second fact that emerged from the conference is that many Black English issues are germane to Black populations throughout the world. The development of effective techniques for teaching a standard language to Blacks who enter schools speaking different languages and/or dialects, while preserving indigenous linguistic systems, is a world need. Virtually all Blacks, including those in Africa, are faced with the task of learning a standardized variety of a European language in order to survive. Interestingly, Blacks in the Caribbean and Africa have probably made more advances in this area than we have in the United States (Alleyne, 1980; Bamgbose, 1976). In order to prevent duplications of effort, research and programs in the area of Black English might well take cognizance of developments in both Africa and the Caribbean.

In response to the international dimension, a World Congress on Black Communication is being planned for Summer, 1981 in Nairobi, Kenya. The subject of Black English, including language education for Black English speakers, will be a major topic of discussion. Proceedings from the Congress will be eventually published in a *Handbook on Black Communication*.

With the impetus provided by the NIE-Ann Arbor conference on Black English, it is reasonable to expect the 1980's to produce considerable research in the area of Black English.

REFERENCES

Alleyne, M.C. *Comparative Afro-American.* Ann Arbor, Michigan: Karoma Publishers, Inc., 1980.

Bamgbose, A. *Mother tongue education: The West African experience.* London: Hodder and Stoughton, 1976.

Bell, R. *Sociolinguistics.* New York: St. Martin's Press, 1976.

Cobbs, P. and Winokur, D. *Education for ethnic and racial diversity.* Bellingham, Washington: Far West Teachers Corps Network, 1977.

Covington, A. Teachers attitudes toward Black English. In Robert L. Williams (Ed.), *Ebonics: The true language of Black folks.* St. Louis: Institute of Black Studies, 1974.

Diop, C.A. *The cultural unity of Black Africa.* Chicago: Third World Press, 1978.

Hoover, M. Characteristics of Black schools at grade level. *The Reading Teacher.* 1978, 757-62.

Hoover, M., Politzer, R. and Taylor, O. *Bias in achievement and diagnostic reading tests: A linguistically oriented view.* Annapolis, Maryland: NIE Conference on Testing, 1975.

Politzer, R. *Teacher workshops, Black English tests for teachers, and selected teaching behaviors and their relation to pupil achievement.* Stanford, California: Center for Educational Research, 1979.

Politzer, R. and Hoover, M. *Teachers' and pupils' attitudes toward Black English speech varieties and Black pupils' achievement* (R & D Memorandum 145). Stanford, California: Stanford Center for Research and Development in Teaching, 1976.

Politzer, R. and Hoover, M. *A field test for Black English tests for teachers* (R & D Memorandum 149) Stanford: Stanford Center for Research and Development in Teaching, 1977.

Politzer, R. and Lewis, S. *The relationship of the Black English tests for teachers and selected teaching behaviors to pupil achievement.* Stanford: Center for Educational Research, 1979.

Taylor, O. Attitudes toward Black and nonstandard English as measured by the language attitude scale. In R. Shuy & R. Fasold. (Eds.), *Language attitudes: Current trends and prospects.* Washington, D.C.: Goergetown University Press, 1973.

Taylor, O. Black English and what to do about it: Some Black community perspectives. In R. Williams (Ed.), *Ebonics: The true language of Black folks.* St. Louis: Institute of Black Studies, 1974.

APPENDIX:

MEMORANDUM OPINION AND ORDER

Charles W. Joiner
United States District Judge

UNITED STATES DISTRICT COURT
EASTERN DISTRICT OF MICHIGAN
SOUTHERN DIVISION

MARTIN LUTHER KING JUNIOR ELEMENTARY)
SCHOOL CHILDREN residing in the Green)
Road Housing Project, and those at that)
scattered site, low income project who)
are or will be eligible to attend that)
Ann Arbor School, including: MICHAEL,)
ANTHONY, GERARD and TYRONE BLAIR, child-)
ren of Annie Blair; TEMKCA S., CHARMIN,)
ROY, and ELISHA BROWNLEE, children of)
Carrie Brownlee; DWAYNE KIHILEE, and)
TITO BRENEN, children of Janice Brenen:)
CAROLYN, GARY, TYRONE and JACQUELINE)
DAVIS, children of Corine Davis; by)
their mothers, and Student Advocacy)
Center as next friends,)
)
        Plaintiffs,)
)
-v-)   Civ. No. <u>77-71861</u>
)
THE MICHIGAN BOARD OF EDUCATION, THE)
MICHIGAN SUPERINTENDENT OF PUBLIC IN-)
STRUCTION, and their employees, agents)
and assignees in their official capa-)
cities; THE ANN ARBOR SCHOOL DISTRICT)
BOARD, THE ANN ARBOR SCHOOL SUPERINTEN-)
DENT HARRY HOWARD; THE ANN ARBOR SCHOOL)
PUPIL PERSONNEL DIRECTOR HAZEL TURNER,)
MARTIN LUTHER KING JUNIOR ELEMENTARY)
SCHOOL PRINCIPAL RACHEL SCHREIBER, and)
their employees, agents, and assignees)
in their official capacities as well as)
named individual Ann Arbor public school)
administrative and teaching personnel)
in their personal capacities,)
)
        Defendants.)
)
)
_____)

MEMORANDUM OPINION AND ORDER

    Plaintiffs are fifteen black preschool or elementary

school children residing at the Green Road Housing Project in

Ann Arbor Michigan, who previously attended, are currently

attending, or will be eligible to attend the Martin Luther

King, Jr., Elementary School. They are suing through their

mothers and the Student Advocacy Center as next friends. The

Student Advocacy Center is a non-profit Michigan corporation

also known as School and Community Services, Inc., with offices

in Ann Arbor, Michigan. In addition to the Michigan Board of

Education and the Ann Arbor School District Board the defen-

dants include the Michigan Superintendent of Public Instruc-
tion, Harry Howard, Hazel Turner, and Rachel Schreiber.
Harry Howard is the Ann Arbor School Superintendent. Hazel
Turner is the Ann Arbor School Pupil Personnel Director.
Rachel Schreiber is the Principal of Martin Luther King,
Jr., Elementary School.

In this lawsuit the plaintiffs allege that in the
process of determining the eligibility of all students for
special education services pursuant to M.C.L.A. 380.1701 et
seq., the defendants have failed to determine whether
plaintiffs' learning difficulties stem from cultural,
social, and economic deprivation and to establish a program
which would enable plaintiffs to overcome the cultural,
social, and economic deprivations which allegedly prevent
them, in varying degrees, from making normal progress in
school. Plaintiffs assert that these omissions constitute
violations of (I) their civil rights protected by 42 U.S.C.
§§1983 and 1985(3), (II) their right to the equal protection
of the laws guaranteed by the Fourteenth Amendment to the
United States Constitution, (III) their right to equal
educational opportunity protected by 20 U.S.C. §§1703(f) and
1706, (IV) their right to the benefits of federal financial
assistance pursuant to 42 U.S.C. §2000(d), (V) their right
to a free education guaranteed by Article 8, Section 2 of
the Michigan Constitution and M.C.L.A. 380.1147, and (VI)
their right to be free from tortious abrogation of their
constitutional rights.

On September 23, 1977, this court denied plaintiffs'
motions for certification as a class and for a preliminary
injunction. The defendants have now moved for the dismissal
of each cause of action alleged in the complaint. The
defendants associated with the City of Ann Arbor have also
moved for the dismissal of the Student Advocacy Center as

next of friend of plaintiffs. For reasons set forth more fully herein, each cause of action alleged in the complaint is dismissed with the exception of the cause of action under 20 U.S.C. §§1703(f) and 1706. In addition, the Student Advocacy Center is dismissed from this case as next friend.

For purposes of deciding defendants' motions to dismiss the well-pleaded allegations of the complaint will be presumed to be true. However, no attempt to give a comprehensive summary of the complaint and its appendices, constituting approximately 180 pages, will be made in this opinion. Rather, a comparatively brief summary of salient points will be sufficient. Plaintiffs are alleged to be culturally, socially, and economically deprived, an allegation which is presumed to be true for purposes of deciding this motion. Five of the fifteen named plaintiffs have been found eligible to receive special education services for the handicapped as hereinafter explained. Four of these children have actually received services. Two children have been classified as "Learning Disabled."[1] Two children have been classified as "Emotionally Impaired." The mother of the fifth child, who is also the mother of one of the learning disabled children, refused any further special services for her other child. There is no separate category or discrete assistance in the program for handicapped for learning difficulties arising from cultural, social, and economic deprivation. Several other plaintiffs have been referred for an evaluation of their eligibility but these referrals have not resulted in any classification or access to services. Plaintiffs do not contend that defendants harbor a racially discriminatory motive for these alleged acts and omissions.

The determination of eligibility for special education

services or "labeling" is governed by Michigan Special Education Code Rules (hereinafter Rule) 340.1701 et seq. promulgated by the State Board of Education pursuant to M.C.L.A. 380.1701 et seq. Commonly, a child will be referred to the special services department by his or her academic teacher for a comprehensive evaluation when that teacher's observations indicate that the child is unable to perform satisfactorily in class. Depending on the nature of the difficulty, the child may be evaluated through standardized tests and interviews by a teacher/consultant, social worker, school psychologist, or even a special diagnostic consultant. Subsequently an "Educational Planning and Placement Committee" (hereinafter EPPC) meeting is held to assess the various evaluations and to recommend a course of action. Rule 340.1701 requires that a representative of the administrative personnel, instructional personnel, diagnostic personnel, and parents of the child involved be in attendance at the EPPC meeting. Furthermore, notice is required to be given to the parent prior to a change in a student's educational status. Rule 340.1723. In the event that a student's parents are not satisfied with the action taken by the EPPC they are entitled to seek administrative review of the decision. Rule 340.1725. Each plaintiff who has received special education services was evaluated and declared eligible for receipt of those services in accordance with the procedures described above. None of the EPPC recommendations pertaining to these children were appealed.

Equal Protection and Civil Rights

From the allegations contained in the complaint it can be deduced with great difficulty that two interrelated theories underlie all of plaintiffs' claims under the Fourteenth Amendment and 42 U.S.C. §§1983 and 1985(3). The evaluation procedures employed by the defendants, pursuant

to the requirements of the Michigan Special Education Code
Rules, are designed to identify children with handicaps.
The Rules do not require and defendants do not provide
special educational services for children whose learning
difficulties are caused solely by cultural, social, and
economic deprivation. Plaintiffs allege that both the
application of defendants' evaluation and special education
procedures and the failure of defendants to provide special
education services for nonhandicapped children suffering
from cultural, social, and economic deprivation creates two
sets of classes of students at King School for purposes of
equal protection analysis. The composition of these classes
varies slightly with the theory being urged by plaintiffs.

1. Theory of Equal Educational Opportunity

According to what will be referred to as the theory of
equal educational opportunity the defendants' evaluation
procedures and special education services which concentrate
only on students with learning difficulties caused by
handicaps are alleged to create one class composed of all
students with learning difficulties who are not culturally,
socially, and economically deprived and another class of all
students with learning difficulties who are culturally,
socially, and economically deprived, i.e., plaintiffs. The
defendants' program is claimed to violate plaintiffs' right
to equal protection of the laws and their civil rights under
42 U.S.C. §§1983 and 1985(3) because it denies special
education services to children whose unsatisfactory academic
performance is based on their cultural, social, or economic
backgrounds and yet provides such services for children
whose unsatisfactory academic performance is based on
handicaps.

No law or clause of the Constitution of the United
States explicitly secures the right of plaintiffs to

special education services to overcome unsatisfactory academic performance based on cultural, social, or economic background. For purposes of an equal protection analysis plaintiffs are not a suspect class. Furthermore, plaintiffs have not identified a fundamental interest which is being infringed by defendants' activities. Education, as important as it may be, has been held not to be a fundamental interest. San Antonio Independent School District et al. v. Rodriguez, 411 U.S. 1 (1972). Therefore, to properly allege a violation of the right to equal protection of the laws plaintiffs must allege that the actions of defendants are not rationally related to a legitimate state purpose.

However, plaintiffs have only alleged that defendants do not provide special education for children whose unsatisfactory academic performance is alleged to be caused by their cultural, social, or economic background. In essence this is a challenge to a limitation put on a measure designed to remedy a problem. It is a challenge to an effort to do good because the remedy adopted did not do good to all. As stated by Justice Brennan in Katzenbach v. Morgan, 384 U.S. 641 (1966), with reference to a federal law which did not restrict or deny the franchise but extended the franchise to persons to whom it would otherwise have been denied by state law:

> In deciding the constitutional propriety of the limitations in such a reform measure we are guided by the familiar principles that a 'statute is not invalid under the Constitution because it might have gone farther than it did,'. . . that a legislature need not 'strike at all evils at the same time,' . . . and that 'reform may take one step at a time, addressing itself to the phase of the problem which seems most acute to the legislative mind.' . . .

Id. at 656-657. See Deal v. Cincinnati Board of Education, 369 F.2d 55, 59-60 (6th Cir. 1966), cert. denied, 389 U.S. 847 (1969). Plaintiffs' theory of equal educational opportunity does not state a claim upon which relief can be granted either pursuant to the Fourteenth Amendment or to 42 U.S.C. §§1983 and 1985(3).

2. Theory of Stigmatization of Defendants

According to what will be referred to as the theory of stigmatization the defendants' evaluation procedures and special education services are alleged to create one class composed of all non-handicapped students who are not culturally, socially, and economically deprived and another class composed of all non-handicapped students who are culturally, socially, and economically deprived, i.e., plaintiffs. The acts complained of are claimed to violate plaintiffs' right to equal protection of the laws because they incorrectly stigmatize plaintiffs as handicapped not only by labeling them but by singling them out from the student body for special treatment. This stigmatization is considered especially grievous in light of the public policy expressed in the Michigan Special Education Code Rules that students whose unsatisfactory scholastic performance is found to be based upon cultural, social, or economic background are not to be considered as handicapped under any category with the possible exception of Emotionally Impaired.

No law or clause of the Constitution of the United States explicitly secures the right to be free from the type of stigmatization alleged. Plaintiffs do not identify themselves as a suspect class for purposes of equal protection analysis. Although plaintiffs all happen to be black the characteristics alleged to identify them as a class are that they are culturally, socially, and economically deprived and are not handicapped. Plaintiffs also do not identify a fundamental interest which is being infringed. Education has been held not to be a fundamental interest.

Rodriguez, supra. Therefore, to properly allege a violation of the right to equal protection of the laws plaintiffs must allege that the diagnostic evaluations and special education undertaken by defendants under color of state law are not rationally related to the legitimate purpose of identifying and assisting handicapped children. See Rodriguez, supra at 54-55.

However, plaintiffs have only alleged that defendants failed to distinguish between learning difficulties caused by cultural, social, and economic deprivation and learning difficulties caused by handicaps, as that word is used in the state statutes, in the process of identifying those students with handicaps. This failure, it is claimed, erroneously includes non-handicapped culturally, socially, and economically deprived students as handicapped. In essence this is an allegation that the class created through the defendants' administration of a special education program for handicapped children is overinclusive. Although this allegation may or may not state a claim for violation of Michigan Special Education Code Rules it does not lead to the conclusion that the procedures employed by defendants are not rationally related to the purpose of assisting handicapped students. On the contrary, the EPPC minutes contained in the appendix to plaintiffs' complaint strongly leads to the inference that defendants' procedures are rationally related to their declared purpose. As stated by Justice Marshall in Rodriguez, supra at 5:

> [T]he existence of 'some inequality' in the manner which the State's rationale is achieved is not alone a sufficient basis for striking down the entire system. McGowan v. Maryland, 366 U.S. 420, 425-426 (1961). It may not be condemned simply because

> it imperfectly effectuate's the State's
> goals. <u>Dandridge</u> v. <u>Williams</u>, 397 U.S., at
> 485. Nor must the financing system fail
> because, as appelles suggest, other methods
> of satisfying the State's interest, which
> occasion 'less drastic' disparities in
> expenditures, might be conceived.

Plaintiffs do not even allege that special education experts have the knowledge or expertise which would enable them accurately to make the distinction between cultural, social, and economic deprivation and handicaps. Furthermore, the EPPC minutes suggest that, contrary to plaintiffs' conclusory allegation, defendants did consider the factor of cultural, social, and economic deprivation and attempted to distinguish such students from students with handicaps.

For these reasons plaintiffs' stigmatization theory does not state a claim upon which relief can be granted either under the Fourteenth Amendment or under 42 U.S.C. §§1983 and 1985(3).

Plaintiffs proceed under this stigmatization theory again to attack the constitutionality of M.C.L.A. 380.1146 which states:

> A separate school or department shall
> not be kept for a person on account of
> race, color, or sex. This section shall
> not be construed to prevent the grading
> of schools according to the intellectual
> progress of the pupil to be taught in sepa-
> rate places as may be deemed expedient.

Plaintiffs claim that since they are all black and since M.C.L.A. §380.1146 permits them to be taught separately from economically advantaged students in the regular education program at King School, thereby stigmatizing plaintiffs, the statute permits unconstitutional discriminatory.

tracking. Since the stigmatization of plaintiffs as
alleged in the complaint does not constitute a violation of the Fourteenth Amendment or 42 U.S. §§1983 and
1985(3) the state statute which permits such stigmatization to occur does not, by virtue of that permission,
violate the constitution.

In support of their stigmatization theory plaintiffs cite the cases of Hobson v. Hanson, 269 F.Supp.
401 (D. D.C. 1967), aff'd Smuck v. Hobson, 408 F.2d 175
(D.C. Cir. 1969); Larry P. v. Riles, 343 F.Supp. 1306
(N.D. Calif. 1972), aff'd, 502 F.2d 963 (9th Cir. 1974);
Board of Education of Cincinnati v. H.E.W., 396 F.Supp. 203,
(S.D. Ohio 1975); Milliken v. Bradley, 97 Sup. Ct. 2749
(1977). In Hobson, unlike the present case, the court found
that the District of Columbia School System was discrimina-
ting against both black and poor persons. In Larry P.
plaintiffs alleged that there was no rational relationship
between the tests used by the school authorities to identify
mentally retarded persons and the goals of the special
education classes for the mentally retarded which had a
disproportionately high percentage of blacks enrolled.
Board of Education of Cincinnati involved a challenge to
HEW's determination that plaintiff was ineligible for
Emergency School Aid Act funds which were sought to enable
emergency desegregation of a school system. In Milliken the
Court approved a portion of the desegregation remedy involving special speech training. Each of these cases is distinguishable from the present case in the critical respect that
they involved racial discrimination, a suspect classification.

Equal Educational Opportunity

In count III of the complaint plaintiffs allege that the

defendants' previously described acts and omissions constitute a failure to take appropriate action to overcome
language barriers in violation of 20 U.S.C. §§1703(f) and
1706.[2] Section 1703(f) of Title 20 of the United States
Code states:

> No State shall deny equal educational oppor-
> tunity to an individual on account of his or
> her race, color, sex, or national origin by --
> (f) the failure by an educational agency
> to take appropriate action to overcome
> language barriers that impede equal partici-
> pation by its students in its instructional
> programs.

Plaintiffs assert that as a class of black economically
disadvantaged children living in the social isolation
of a housing project they speak a vernacular of English,
referred to as "Black English", which is so different from
the English commonly spoken in the public schools as to
constitute a language barrier which impedes their equal
participaiton in King School's instructional programs.

In their attack on the legal sufficiency of this
claim defendants present two issues for resolution. The
first issue is whether the existence of a dual school system
is prerequisite to the finding of a denial of equal educational opportunity under section 1703(f). The second issue
is whether the term "language barrier" can be interpreted to
include a child's inability to use standard English effectively because that child's native language is what plaintiffs have termed "Black English" as opposed to a foreign
language such as Spanish.

1. Dual School System Argument

The Equal Educational Opportunities Act of 1974 origin-
ated as a message from President Nixon to Congress on school

busing. 118 Cong. Rec. 8928 (1972).[3] The President's proposal proceeded on a frequently stated presumption that
"[t]he years since Brown v. Board of Education have been
ones of dismantling the old dual school system in these
areas where it existed -- a process that has now been substantially completed." Given this presumption the President wanted
to shift the focus of efforts to achieve racial equality from
more busing to better education. 118 Cong. Rec. 8929 (1972).
To achieve this shift the President's proposal was designed "to
give the courts a new and broader base on which to decide
future cases and to place the emphasis where it belongs: on
better education for all our children" and to set forth alternatives to the busing remedy. 118 Cong. Rec. 8931 (1972). The
essence of what is now 20 U.S.C. §1703 was then the President's
definition of the denial of equal educational opportunity which
constituted the "broader base on which to decide future cases."
The President described this broader base as setting "standards for all school districts throughout the Nation, as the
basic requirements for carrying out, in the field of public
education, the Constitutional guarantee that each person
shall have equal protection of the laws." 118 Cong. Rec.
8931 (1972).

From these remarks it appears that the President was
proposing legislation which would not merely shift the focus
of the courts from busing to other remedies for racially
segregated "dual school systems" but which would actually
create statutory definitions of equal educational opportunity broader than the standards thus far formulated by the
courts when interpreting the equal protection clause of the
Fourteenth Amendment. In a sense these statutory standards
would constitute a new definition of dual school system.

The theme of this message to Congress is reflected both in the report of the Committee on Education and Labor which recommended passage of the bill and in the language and structure of the Act itself. The Committee on Education and Labor, which reported on the Equal Educational Opportunities Act of 1972 bill to the House of Representatives with the recommendation that it pass, stated:

> [T]o assist in that final elimination [of dejure segregation] the committee bill for the first time in Federal Law contains an illustrative definition of denial of equal educational opportunity. It is the purpose of that definition . . . to provide school and governmental authorities with a clear delineation of their responsibilities to their students and employees and to provide the students and employees with the means to achieve enforcement of their rights.

H.R. Rep. No. 1335, 92d Cong., 2d Sess. 3 (1972). The illustrative definition to which the committee report refers is Title II of the EEOA which defines unlawful practices including the failure to eliminate language barriers. 20 U.S.C. §1703(f). Furthermore, Section 1701 of Title 20 of the United States Code, the policy and purpose section of the EEOA, states in pertinent part:

> (a) The Congress declares it to be the policy of the United States that --
> (1) all children enrolled in public schools are entitled to equal educational opportunity without regard to race, color, sex, or national origin . . .

This language confirms that the expansive definitions of equal educational opportunity are a matter of policy and not merely questionable restatements of preexisting case law on equal protection.

Most of the cases interpreting 20 U.S.C. §1701 et seq., are desegregation cases in which no consideration whatsoever is given to whether the existence of a dual school system is a prerequisite to the enforcement of rights established under §1703. There are, however, two cases

which provide support for the proposition that the existence of a dual school system is not a prerequisite. In
U.S. v. Hinds County School Board et al., 560 F.2d 619
(5th Cir. 1977) the court held that a sex segregated school
assignment violated §1703(a). Although the Hinds County
School Board had previously been found to operate a dual
school system with respect to blacks, no discrimination had
ever been alleged to exist with respect to women. The court
pointed out that in 20 U.S.C. §1703 Congress went "beyond
the acts and practices proscribed prior to the EEOA's
passage and [guaranteed] additional rights to public school
children." Hinds, supra at 624.

In Evans v. Buchanan et al., 416 F. Supp. 328 (D.
Del. 1976), the court granted a motion to intervene brought
by Hispanics who sought to protect their bilingual program
from being elimated in a court ordered desegregation plan
aimed at black-white segregation. No discrimination with
respect to Hispanics had been alleged in that case. The
court held that the Hispanic intervenor's right to a bilingual program was protected by 20 U.S.C. §1703(f).

Given the nature of the legislative history and the
language and structure of the statute itself it does not
appear that the existence of a dual school system, in the
sense that term has heretofore been used by courts to denote
a school system which is racially segregated in violation of
the Fourteenth Amendement, is prerequisite to a finding that
a provision of the EEOA of 1974 has been violated.

   2. No Foreign Language Barrier Argument

Federal Courts have not explicitly addressed the issue
of whether the language barrier specified in §1703(f) must
be a foreign language barrier or may also include the
barrier standard English presents to a black child with a
"Black English" background. Section 1703(f) states only that

> No State shall deny equal educational
> opportunity to an individual on account of
> his or her race, color, sex, or national
> origin, by --
> f) the failure by an educational agency to
> take appropriate action to overcome language
> barriers that impede equal participation by
> its students in its instructional programs.

This section (f) requires a showing of two things. (1) The denial of educational opportunity must be on "account of" race, color, sex or national origin and, (2) the educational agency must fail to take action to overcome language barriers that are sufficiently severe so as to impede a student's equal participation in instructional programs. So the allegations in this case must be examined to determine the seriousness of the language barriers and the cause of the alleged denial of educational opportunities that results from the failure to take action to overcome the language barriers.

The statutory language places no limitation on the character or source of the language barrier except that it must be serious enough to "impede equal participation by . . . students in . . . instructional programs." Barring any more explicit legislative guidance to the contrary §1703(f) applies to language barriers of appropriate severity encountered by students who speak "Black English" as well as to language barriers encountered by students who speak German.

The legislative history of this section does not provide a meaning more specific or limited in scope than the language of the statute. In his message to Congress President Nixon stated:

> School authorities must take appropriate
> action to overcome whatever language barriers
> might exist, in order to enable all students
> to participate equally in educational
> programs. This would establish, in effect,
> an educational bill of rights for Mexican-
> Americans, Puerto Ricans, Indians and others
> who start under language handicaps, and
> ensure at last that they too would have
> equal opportunity. [Emphasis added]

162

118 Cong. Rec. 8931 (1972). The President's list of persons covered by his proposal is not only merely illustrative but could well include students whose "language barrier" results from the use of some type of nonstandard English. The report of the House Committee on Education and Labor simply paraphrases the statutory language and commends HEW for having initiated a compliance review of school districts throughout the country to ascertain whether they have fulfilled their obligation to remove language and cultural barriers under Title VI of the Civil Rights Act of 1964. H. R. Rep. No. 1335, 92d Cong., 2d Sess. 6 (1972).

Paragraph 120 of the complaint contains an allegation that plaintiffs are all Black and economically disadvantaged and that the defendants have failed to take appropriate action to overcome language barriers. There is enough stated implicitly in this allegation as to causation to prevent this court from granting a motion to dismiss. In keeping with the terms of the statute this court holds that allegations of failure by an educational agency to take appropriate action to overcome language barriers of students which impede their equal participation in instructional programs when tied, as alleged, to race allege a violation of 20 U.S.C. §1703(f). Defendants' motion to dismiss plaintiffs claim under 20 U.S.C. §1703(f) in count III of their complaint is denied.

Benefits of Federal Financial Assistance

Plaintiffs' fourth cause of action is based on 42 U.S.C. §2000d which provides:

> No person in the United States shall, on the ground of race, color, or national origin, be excluded from participation in, be denied the benefits of, or be subjected to discrimination under any program or activity receiving Federal financial assistance.

In paragraph 123 of their complaint Plaintiffs state:

> They specifically are being denied numerous benefits under Title 20 of the United States Code, because they are at a school where too few economically disadvantage children attended to warrant the provision of special programs to service these named plaintiff children . . . (Emphasis added.)

The statute provides that no person shall be denied benefits on the ground of race, color or national origin. Plaintiffs allege that they are being denied benefits because there are too few economically disadvantaged students at King School. Even assuming that benefits were being denied, plaintiffs' allegation fails to state a claim under 42 U.S.C.§2000d since they have failed to allege that the benefits were being denied on the grounds prohibited by 42 U.S.C. §2000(d). Furthermore, plaintiffs' allegations relative to language barriers are adequately addressed under plaintiffs' third alleged cause of action. Therefore, plaintiffs' fourth cause of action is dismissed for failure to state a claim upon which relief may be granted.

Free Education

In count V of the complaint plaintiffs claim that their right to a free education, guaranteed by Article 8, Section 2 of the Michigan Constitution and M.C.L.A. 380.1147(1), has been violated to the extent that defendants have failed to provide appropriate special education services thus allowing plaintiffs to become illiterate. Article 8, Section 2 of the Michigan Constitution states:

> The legislature shall maintain and support a system of free public elementary and secondary schools as defined by law . . .

Section 380.1147(1) of Michigan Compiled Laws Annotated states:

> (1)   A person, resident of a school district not maintaining a kindergarten and at least 5 years of age on the first day of enrollment of the school year, shall have a right to attend school in the district.
>
> (2)   In a school district where provision is made for kindergarten work, a child, resident of the district, is entitled to enroll in the kindergarten if the child is at least 5 years of age on December 1 of the school year of enrollment. In a school district which has semi-annual promotions, a child, resident of the district, is entitled to enroll in kindergarten for the second semester if the child is at least 5 years of age on March 1 of the year of enrollment.

Plaintiffs claim their right to free education is violated since they are not getting books and materials relied upon by King School teachers to prepare other children, such as reading materials available in the homes of middle and higher income students. Plaintiffs also state that they are being denied equal educational opportunity under Michigan law. Article 8, Section 2 of the Michigan Constitution and M.C.L.A. 380.1147(1) do not explicitly require that public school systems provide such special educational services for culturally, socially, and economically deprived students. Plaintiffs cite Bond v. Ann Arbor School District, 383 Mich. 694 (1970), in support of their proposition. The plaintiffs in Bond sought to have the Court declare book, materials, and activities fees collected by the Ann Arbor Public Schools violative of the Michigan Constitution, Art. 8, Sec. 2. The Court held that by applying either the "necessary elements of any school's activity" test or the "integral fundamental part of the elementary and secondary education" test, it was clear that books and school supplies were an essential part of a system of free public elementary and secondary schools. Bond,

supra at 702. A fair reading of this opinion indicates that
the Court did not mean to include in its holding any materials which could possibly be useful in the educational
process. They meant textbooks and supplies or equipment
used in school.

The opinion in Governor v. State Treasurer, 390 Mich.
389 (1973), contains language which suggests not only that
the Michigan Constitution does not mandate equal educational
opportunity as claimed by plaintiffs but also that the scope
of the Michigan equal protection clause tracks that of the
federal constitution with the result that the defendants'
failure to provide plaintiffs with compensatory services and
their placement of plaintiffs in special education classes
does not violate plaintiffs' Michigan equal protection rights
just as those acts and omissions do not violate plaintiffs'
federal equal protection rights. The Court stated:

> [T]he state's obligation to provide a system
> of public schools is not the same as the
> claimed obligation to provide equality of
> educational opportunity. Because of defini-
> tional difficulties and differences in
> educational philosophy and student ability,
> motivation, background, etc., no system of
> public schools can provide equality of
> educational opportunity in all its diverse
> dimensions. All that can properly be
> expected of the state is that it maintain
> and support a system of public schools that
> furnishes adequate educational services to
> all children. (Emphasis added)

Governor, supra at 406. Furthermore the Court noted that in
the past it had frequently held that the Michigan Constitution
secures the same right of equal protection as the federal
constitution. Although the Court expressly reserved the issue
of whether education is a fundamental interest in Michigan the
Court's views on equal educational opportunity strongly suggest
that it would not be sympathetic to plaintiffs' claims. Given
this posture of Michigan case law plaintiffs have failed to
state a cause of action upon which relief can be granted.

Tortious Abrogation of Constitutional Rights

Since plaintiffs' claims for violation of their various constitutional rights have all been dismissed for failure to state a claim upon which relief can be granted they cannot continue to maintain an action sounding in tort for willful or reckless violation of those rights by certain named defendants. Therefore, plaintiffs' sixth cause of action in tort against Hazel Turner and Rachel Schreiber and certain of their agents and employees for willful or reckless violation of plaintiffs' constitutional rights is dismissed for failure to state a claim upon which relief can be granted.

Student Advocacy Center as Next Friend

The Ann Arbor defendants, pursuant to F.R.C.P. 9(a), have raised the issue of the capacity of the Student Advocacy Center to act as next friend to plaintiff school children. The capacity of a representative to sue is to be determined by the law of the state in which the district court is held under F.R.C.P. 17(c).[4] Slade v. Louisiana Power & Light Co., 418 F.2d 125 (5th Cir. 1969). The Michigan rule, GCR, 1963, 201.5(2) provides in pertinent part:

> Appointment of next friend . . . shall be made by the court: . . . (2) in the case of an infant party under the age of 14 years or an incompetent party, upon the nomination of the next of kin of such party . . . The court in its discretion may refuse to appoint any representative deemed unsuitable. . .

The next of kin in this case are the mothers of the various plaintiffs who are also identified as next friend in the complaint. Michigan infants with living parents have sued through a non-parent next of friend appointed under this rule. In Buckholz v. Leveille, 37 Mich. App. 166 (1971), a 16 year old high school student was held to be entitled to bring suit attacking the constitutionality of a school dress code even though his parents agreed with the dress code and desired that the suit be dismissed. However, beyond the language of the rule, which by implication contemplates only one next friend, there are no cases which give guidance on the permissibility of multiple next friends.

Aside from the language of the rule there is an important reason for limiting the number of next friends to one individual or entity. The next friend is charged with the responsibility of representing an infant or incompetent person in a lawsuit. The existence of multiple next friends creates a potential for conflict of opinion and action which is a serious, if not overwhelming, impediment to the progress of a lawsuit and to responsible representation. For this reason Michigan G.C.R., 1963, 201.5(2) and F.R.C.P. 17(c) are held to authorize a court, in its discretion, to limit an appointment to only one next friend. In this case it appears most appropriate to permit the mother of each plaintiff school child to continue as next friend and to dismiss the Student Advocacy Center from the lawsuit as next friend. This holding does not in any way prevent the Student Advocacy Center from providing such assistance to plaintiffs as they desire to accept. It does, however, vest the ultimate responsibility for the representation of each plaintiff school child in one individual.

In summary, plaintiffs' claims for violation of their rights under the Fourteenth Amendment to the Constitution, 42 U.S.C. §§1983 and 1985(3), 42 U.S.C. §2000d, Article 8, Section 2 of the Michigan Constitution, M.C.L.A. 380.1147(1), and the common law are all dismissed for failure to state a claim upon which relief can be granted. In addition, the Student Advocacy Center is dismissed from this lawsuit as next friend since the rules authorizing appointment of next friends authorize the court, in its discretion, to limit an appointment to only one next friend. Defendants' motion to dismiss plaintiffs' claim for violation of their rights under 20 U.S.C. §§1703(f) and 19706 is denied.

So Ordered.

Charles N. Joiner
_____
United States District Judge

Dated: May 17, 1978
       Detroit, Michigan

FOOTNOTES

[1] The handicap category of Learning Disabled is specifically defined to exclude all students whose unsatisfactory performance is found to be based upon social, economic, or cultural background as are all other categories of handicap with the exception of Emotionally Impaired. Rule 340.1713(13)(e).

[2] Section 1706 of Title 20 of the United States Code states:

> An individual denied an equal educational opportunity as defined by this subchapter may institute a civil action in an appropriate district court of the United States against such parties, and for such relief, as may be appropriate. . . .

[3] In 1974, during House debate on HR 69, a bill to extend and amend the Elementary and Secondary Education Act of 1965, Representative Esch proposed an amendment identical in relevant portions with the Equal Educational Opportunities Act of 1972 (hereinafter EEOA). 20 U.S.C. §1701 et seq. This amendment was passed by the House but defeated in the Senate in 1972. The amendment was adopted and after modifications in the Senate, not relevant to this discussion, the EEOA was enacted into law. As a result there were no committee hearings conducted on the measure during the 93d session of Congress. 1974 U.S. Code Congress. 1974 U.S. Code Cong. & Admin. Newsa 4206. However, there were extensive hearings held on the EEOA in 1972. The legislative deliberations on this measure in 1972 form the basis for the discussion of legislative history in this opinion.

[4] Rule 17(c) of the Federal Rules of Civil Procedure states:

> INFANTS OR INCOMPETENT PERSONS. Whenever an infant or incompetent person has a representative, such as a general guardian, committee, conservator, or other like fiduciary, the representative may sue or defend on behalf of the infant or incompetent person. If an infant or incompetent person does not have a duly appointed representative he may sue by his next friend or by a guardian ad litem for an infant or incompetent person not otherwise represented in an action or shall make such other order as it deems proper for the protection of the infant or incompetent person.